A lot has been written about international financial centres in the last 20 years. J. J. Woo goes one step further, combining sophisticated conceptualisation with vivid depiction in order to explain the phenomenal rise of Singapore in the late 20th and early 21st century. The result of the triple process of globalisation, financialisation, and centralisation, Singapore is at once a unique success story and part of the broader transformation of the world of finance, from the local to the global. *3-in-1: Governing a Global Financial Centre* will be of interest to an equally wide readership, from academics to policy-makers.

Youssef Cassis
Professor of Economic History,
European University Institute,
and Joint Chair, Department of History
and Civilisation, and Robert Schuman Centre
for Advanced Studies

As cities become as much local as global, we need frameworks such as J. J. Woo's that capture the economic, social and political drivers that make a city such as Singapore a unique global financial center. This book is an important contribution to the theory and practice of political economy.

Parag Khanna
Senior Research Fellow, Lee Kuan Yew School of Public Policy
and author, *Connectography: Mapping the Future of Global Civilization*

Singapore is the world's third leading financial center behind only London and New York. This fascinating book provides an overview of Singapore's success by focusing on three factors that have driven this process: globalisation, financialisation, and centralisation. The book considers not only economic factors but also a wider set of sociopolitical forces. This book is timely and will be of great interest to a wide spectrum of readers — academics, policymakers, students of development economics, and the general public.

Pradumna Bickram Rana
Associate Professor and Coordinator of the International Political Economy Programme
Nanyang Technological University (NTU), Singapore

3-in-1: Governing a Global Financial Centre is a welcome addition to the literature on creating an internationally competitive center of excellence in the globally competitive world of financial services. This is the third in a trilogy of books by Professor J. J. Woo on Singapore's remarkable emergence as a global financial center, and is both a distillation and synthesis of Professor Woo's research to date. However, whereas the first two volumes were targeted primarily at academics, this book is intended to reach a much wider audience, so it is accessible to specialists and non-specialists alike. Many of the book's findings are unexpected and counter-intuitive, given Singapore's reputation as an extremely successful but relatively risk-averse international business hub. Especially enlightening are Professor Woo's focus on Singapore's embrace of globalisation, financialisation, and centralisation, as well as his broad, inclusive concept of what constitutes a financial sector. This is a must read for anyone interested in understanding what it takes to become a successful global financial centre, and how policymakers can help to place a city on this often elusive trajectory.

Jay K. Rosengard
Director, Financial Sector Program
Harvard Kennedy School, Harvard University

3-in-1

Governing a Global Financial Centre

3-in-1
Governing a Global Financial Centre

J. J. Woo

Nanyang Technological University, Singapore

Harvard University, USA

World Scientific

NEW JERSEY • LONDON • SINGAPORE • BEIJING • SHANGHAI • HONG KONG • TAIPEI • CHENNAI • TOKYO

Published by

World Scientific Publishing Co. Pte. Ltd.
5 Toh Tuck Link, Singapore 596224
USA office: 27 Warren Street, Suite 401-402, Hackensack, NJ 07601
UK office: 57 Shelton Street, Covent Garden, London WC2H 9HE

Library of Congress Cataloging-in-Publication Data
Names: Woo, J. J. (Jun Jie), author.
Title: 3-in-1 : governing a global financial centre / J.J. Woo.
Other titles: Three in one
Description: New Jersey : World Scientific, [2017] | Includes bibliographical references.
Identifiers: LCCN 2017010485 | ISBN 9789813221161 (hardcover)
Subjects: LCSH: Financial services industry--Singapore. | Financial institutions, International--Singapore. | International finance--Political aspects--Singapore.
Classification: LCC HG187.S55 .W66 2017 | DDC 332/.042095957--dc23
LC record available at https://lccn.loc.gov/2017010485

British Library Cataloguing-in-Publication Data
A catalogue record for this book is available from the British Library.

Desk Editor: Karimah Samsudin

Printed in Singapore by B & Jo Enterprise Pte Ltd

To the two great cities of Boston and Singapore,
where this book was conceived and written

And as always, to Debbie

Contents

Acknowledgements

This book would not have been possible without the love and support of my wife, Debbie, whose inputs and ideas, floated across our dinner table and over our many coffee dates, have helped make me become a better writer.

During the course of writing this book, I was a Rajawali Fellow at the Ash Center for Democratic Governance and Innovation, Harvard Kennedy School. I am therefore deeply indebted to the Center, especially Dr Kaori Urayama, for providing me with a collegial and intellectually stimulating environment, and Nanyang Technological University, for providing me with the necessary resources for my research.

Indeed, this book bears the imprint of these two great institutions — Harvard University and Nanyang Technological University — and the vibrant research communities that they host.

As always, I am thankful for the presence of family and friends who have kept me company and in good cheer. These include my parents and sister, G. Nandhakumar, Daniel Ouyang, Simon Pang, Ong Shun Wei and Jamie Chung, Alfred Pang,

Gregory Tan, S.J., Joseph Simmons, S.J., Benjamin Goh, and all at the Singapore Policy Journal.

Last but by no means least, I am highly grateful to my editor, Ms Karimah Samsudin, for her all assistance and advice in the preparation of this manuscript. It is a joy for any author to be working with an editor of such capability and professionalism.

About the Book

3-in-1: Governing a Global Financial Centre provides a comprehensive understanding of Singapore's past development and future success as a global financial centre. It focuses on three transformational processes that have determined the city-state's financial sector development and governance — globalisation, financialisation, and centralisation — and their impacts across three areas: the economy, governance, and technology. More importantly, this book takes a multidimensional approach by considering the inter-related and interdependent nature of these three transformational processes. Just like the 3-in-1 coffee mix that is such a ubiquitous feature of everyday life in Singapore, the individual ingredients of Singapore's success as a global financial centre do not act alone, but as an integrated whole that manifests itself in one final product: the global financial centre.

Preface

This book was conceived as the third of a trilogy of books that have focused on Singapore's development as a global financial centre.

While the first book, *Business and Politics in Asia's Key Financial Centre: Hong Kong, Singapore and Shanghai*, had discussed Singapore's position as a leading Asian financial centre *vis-à-vis* its regional competitors, the second book, *Singapore as an International Political Economy: History, Politics, and Policy*, had focused on the historical, spatial, political and policy aspects of financial sector development in Singapore.

In contrast to these two earlier works, which were more research-focused, this book provides a broader discussion that seeks to avoid research jargon and provide instead a more accessible account of the underlying processes that have driven Singapore's success as a global financial centre. In a sense, it is an attempt to consolidate the findings of my earlier work.

In doing so, it recognises the ways in which major socio-economic-political processes such as globalisation, financialisation and centralisation often converge upon a city. More importantly, this book argues that a city's ability to transform itself into a vibrant and successful global financial centre hinges on the ability of its leaders and policymakers to manage these processes and direct them towards positive policy outcomes.

Hopefully, this book contributes to existing understandings of how global financial centres emerge and thrive, and how policymakers can contribute towards the transformation of a city into a successful global financial centre.

J. J. Woo
28 January 2017
Boston, Singapore

OVER 100 YEARS AGO, THIS WAS A MUD-FLAT, SWAMP. TODAY, THIS IS A MODERN CITY. TEN YEARS FROM NOW, THIS WILL BE A METROPOLIS. NEVER FEAR.

LEE KUAN YEW
SPEECH AT THE SREE NARAYANA MISSION
12 SEPTEMBER 1965

CHAPTER ONE

The Political Economy of a Global Financial Centre

As conduits of global capital flows and geospatial sites for the convergence of money and power, global financial centres have become an important focus of research and analysis for economists, political scientists, and urban scholars alike. While earlier efforts to understand the formation and development of global financial centres were situated within the disciplinary confines of economics,[1] subsequent efforts have since expanded beyond the theoretical ambit of economics to address the social, political, and urban-spatial aspects of an international financial centre (IFC).[2]

There is, in other words, a growing appreciation of the social, political, and spatial contexts within which global financial centres are embedded.[3] Indeed, a financial centre is essentially a nexus for the confluence of global capital, power, and financial labour. Furthermore, most, if not all, leading financial centres are housed within global cities and enmeshed within the sociopolitical fabric of the city. Global financial centres are therefore deeply urban in nature and strongly rooted within their sociopolitical-spatial contexts.

However, this is a point that has largely eluded economists, who are more interested in the economic gains and implications of establishing a financial centre. What have emerged from this conceptual void are efforts by geographers and political scientists to provide a greater contextual nuance in the understanding of global financial centres.[4] Furthermore, sustained economic growth in Asia has given rise to the emergence of Asian financial centres that are situated within unique sociopolitical-economic systems and which require closer analysis. One of these leading Asian financial centres is Singapore.

From its independence as a sovereign state, Singapore has sought to establish itself as a global hub for financial services by leveraging on its favourable time zone and strategic location within a thriving Asia Pacific region. It has largely been successful, having been ranked consistently among the top competitive financial centres of the world.[5] More importantly, this drive to become a global financial centre has necessitated a mobilisation of Singapore's social, economic, and political resources.

As a consequence, Singapore's role and identity as a global financial centre is deeply informed by its social, economic, political and geospatial circumstances. This book focuses on this multifaceted aspect of Singapore's current position and future prospects as a leading global financial centre. In analysing a multifaceted phenomenon or object, disciplinary eclecticism is necessary. In light of this necessity, and informed by my own theoretical training, this book will take an international political economy approach.

This chapter will provide the conceptual framing for the rest of this book. It does so by focusing on transformational processes that have driven the world's leading global financial centres: (1) globalisation, (2) financialisation, and (3) centralisation or agglomeration. Taken together, these three processes form, both metaphorically and literally, a global financial centre. In delineating these three processes, this chapter is therefore also an exercise in conceptually disaggregating a global financial centre into its constituent parts (or in this case, processes).

However, these three processes do not operate in isolation. Rather, they are deeply intertwined, with their individual impacts on Singapore's development as a global financial centre not always clearly distinguishable. As the saying goes, the result is far greater than a sum of its parts. As this book will show, it is Singapore's ability to manage these three intermingled processes in a coherent and integrative manner that has contributed to its success.

It is also important to note that all three processes involve sociopolitical forces, not simply economic ones. This goes to reiterate this book's core underlying assumption that global financial centres are not simply economic, but also social, political, and spatial phenomena. By distinguishing between the three processes, this chapter also seeks to avoid the well-trodden (and certainly well-meaning) but clichéd approach of taking on different theoretical lenses (economics, politics, geography, etc.) Instead, it addresses *all* these lenses within each process. Perhaps more importantly, it does so through a more nuanced and integrated manner that recognises the messy reality that is financial sector governance.

Globalisation

The first process, globalisation, has left an indelible mark on the ways that societies are organised and economies governed, although it has not done so without some controversy.[6] In particular, globalisation has led to heightened economic interdependency among states and as a consequence, an increasingly dense web of economic and financial relations. Of specific interest to this book is financial globalisation, which has been defined as the "global linkages through cross-border financial flows".[7]

Financial globalisation, in other words, has something to do with the increasing integration of financial markets, facilitated (or exacerbated) by forces of globalisation. The benefits, and costs, of financial globalisation, particularly to developing economies, are well documented.[8] Specifically, financial centre development has been positively associated with economic growth,[9] although financial risks and contagion magnify with financial globalisation as well, as the 2007 global financial crisis (GFC) has shown.

Either ways, globalisation was, from the beginning, a crucial driving force behind Singapore's developmental trajectory as a global financial centre. The possibility of establishing a financial sector in Singapore was first raised by then economic advisor Albert Winsemius, who had noted that Singapore's time zone could potentially allow it to exploit a gap in trading hours among various financial centres. There was therefore already, in 1965, an inkling of the opportunities that could arise from tapping into an increasingly globalised economy.

This placed Singapore squarely within an ongoing global dialogue on 'global cities' and their roles as 'command centres' of the global economy.[10] Yet, it would be misleading to say that the notion of Singapore as a global city only took root in 2003. Indeed, former Minister for Foreign Affairs S. Rajaratnam had, in as early as 1972, characterised Singapore as a 'global city' that could draw on the rest of the world as its 'hinterland'.[11] Singapore has therefore been seen as a global city even before the emergence of the global city as theoretical construct and analytical category in the 2000s.

Financialisation

At broadly the same time that national economies were becoming increasingly globalised and intertwined with each other, there was a second process that was shaping the ways in which economies are structured. This process is broadly known as 'financialisation'. Financialisation has been broadly defined as the "increasing role of financial motives, financial markets, financial actors, and financial institutions in the operation of domestic and international economies".[12] What this often means is that financial services are increasingly becoming prioritised over non-financial economic activities.

More than simply a shift from 'real' economic activities such as manufacturing and trade to financial activities, financialisation has been associated with the permeation of finance into every aspect of economic, social, and political life.[13] What this means is that financialisation cuts across the various modalities of society, posing social, economic, political, and urban implications. With the growing influence of financial firms and the emergence of social categories such as the 'financial subject' or 'financial citizen', finance has permeated into many aspects of political decision-making and citizenship.

Given its position as a small open economy and its desire to become a leading global financial centre, Singapore is not exempt from the forces and pressures of financialisation. As of 2014, the financial services sector accounts for 12.5% of Singapore's GDP and continues to register strong growth. For instance, the asset management industry grew by 7.7% while the overall services sector grew by 3.2% in 2014.[14] In stark contrast, manufacturing contracted by 6% in that same year. Indeed, the manufacturing sector's share of GDP has steadily declined from 27.7% in 2000 to 18.4% in 2014.[15]

These figures reflect a steady decline in manufacturing, coupled with strong growth in financial services. Broadly speaking, Singapore is experiencing the sort of financialisation that many other cities and countries are facing as well, with the financial services sector growing at the expense of real economic activities. However, and is often the case, statistics do not tell the whole story. The financialisation that Singapore has experienced over the past few decades is in fact qualitatively different from that in other countries.

First and foremost, both economic and financial sector development remain largely state-led, under the purview of semi-autonomous statutory agencies such as the Economic Development Board (EDB) and the Monetary Authority of Singapore (MAS). As a consequence of this state-led approach, the growth and prioritisation of Singapore's financial services sector is really part of the government's efforts to capitalise on financial services as an engine for economic growth.[16] The intrusion of financial sector demands and motivations into the state's economic policy decisions therefore derives from the government's pragmatic desire to seek out new sources of growth and revenue for the fledgling nation-state.[17]

Making Sure the Centre Holds

While the forces of globalisation and financialisation have been associated with the spatial decentralisation of economic processes and activities, the reality is that financial activities remain concentrated within a select group of global financial centres.[18] Economists have described this tendency for financial activities to coalesce around a physical location as 'agglomeration' or 'clustering'.[19] Of particular importance to such clustering of financial activities is the availability of supporting services such as accounting and legal services.

Financial centralisation therefore acts as a crucial counterbalance to financial globalisation and financialisation, with the global financial centre placed at the confluence of these three processes and therefore sustained by the tensions between them. The desire of cities to become successful global financial centres paradoxically depends upon a straddling of global financial flows and local infrastructural conditions. Centralisation, in other words, places the city front and centre in the study of global financial centres.

Effectively the world's only functioning sovereign city-state, Singapore is the archetypal case study of a global financial centre in a global city. It owes its economic sustenance almost entirely to its ability to attract and consolidate global economic and financial flows by ensuring a conducive business environment. Indeed, clustering is a key strategy that has sustained Singapore's economic growth over the decades, beginning with its early efforts to encourage the setting up of regional offices by multinational corporations (MNCs) within its borders.[20]

More importantly, and as I have alluded above, there is a significant extent of centralised policymaking in Singapore's economic and financial sector development. Centralisation, in other words, involves both the agglomeration of economic activity and the consolidation of state power. Through this dual process of centralisation, Singapore has been able to consolidate itself, both economically and politically, in its efforts to become a cohesive global financial centre and global city. This has imbued it with a significant extent of nimbleness as it navigates the global political economy.

3-in-1

There is therefore a need to understand the ways in which these three processes — globalisation, financialisation, and centralisation — have impacted Singapore's transformation and development into a successful global financial centre. More importantly, there is a need to recognise that these three processes are in reality deeply intertwined and even interdependent. As Chapter 5 will discuss, the governance of a global financial centre is more complex, and certainly far messier, than existing research and studies on financial centres make it out to be.

As Chapters 2 to 4 show, financial sector development is a phenomenon that cuts across disciplinary and conceptual boundaries, often giving rise to significant implications for the social, political, urban, and even cultural life of a city, aside from its economic prospects. While Chapters 2 to 4 each provide an individual analysis of globalisation, financialisation, and centralisation, the reality, as Chapter 5 will show, is that these three processes do not simply constitute individual ingredients in Singapore's financial sector development.

Rather, they often blend into each other, manifesting and converging onto a singular final product: the global financial centre. Hence, like the pre-mixed coffee products that one is bound to find in a typical Singaporean supermarket (i.e., the

'3-in-1' coffee mix), the global financial centre is also a '3-in-1' phenomenon, formed by a complex mix of globalisation, financialisation, and centralisation, with its success driven not by the presence of any one of these three processes, but a well-mixed blend of all three.

Conclusion

This chapter has provided a conceptual framework, with which the rest of this book will be structured. Specifically, I have conceptually delineated a global financial centre into three transformational processes: globalisation, financialisation, and centralisation. These three processes have driven Singapore's emergence as a global financial centre, and continues to sustain the city-state's position among the world's top financial centres.

These three transformations will therefore be discussed separately in the following chapters, with Chapter 2 focusing on globalisation, Chapter 3 on financialisation, and Chapter 4 on centralisation. Each chapter will also discuss the three major forces that drive each process: economic, sociopolitical, and technological forces. The goal of these three chapters is to provide a conceptual understanding of these three processes and discuss the ways in which they have determined and shaped financial sector development and governance in Singapore.

This is followed by Chapter 5, which discusses how these three processes converge upon the global financial centre, and how Singapore has managed and even leveraged upon this confluence of the three forces of globalisation, financialisation, and centralisation to transform itself into a successful and thriving global financial centre. This chapter also serves as a conclusion, by discussing future trajectories and the policy implications of governing a "3-in-1" global financial centre.

Endnotes

1. Charles P. Kindleberger, The Formation of Financial Centers: A Study in Comparative Economic History (*Princeton Studies in International Finance* No. 36),

1st edition (New Jersey: Princeton University Press, 1974); Richard Roberts, ed., *International Financial Centres* (Edward Elgar Pub, 1994); Howard Curtis Reed, *The Preeminence of International Financial Centers* (New York: Praeger, 1981).

2. J. J. Woo, *Business and Politics in Asia's Key Financial Centres — Hong Kong, Singapore and Shanghai*, 1st ed., Springerbriefs in Finance (Singapore: Springer, 2016); Karen P. Y. Lai and Choon Hang Tan, "'Neighbours First, Bankers Second': Mobilising Financial Citizenship in Singapore," *Geoforum* 64 (August 2015): 65–77; Saskia J. Sassen, *Cities in a World Economy*, 4th edition (California: SAGE Publications, Inc, 2011); Saskia Sassen, "Global Financial Centers," *Foreign Affairs* 78 (1999): 75–87; Roger Lee and Ulrich Schmidt-Marwede, "Interurban Competition? Financial Centres and the Geography of Financial Production*," *International Journal of Urban and Regional Research* 17, No. 4 (1993): 492–515.
3. J. J. Woo, *Singapore as an International Financial Centre: History, Politics and Policy* (London: Palgrave Macmillan, 2016).
4. Philip G. Cerny, "The Political Economy of International Finance," in *Finance and World Politics: Markets, Regimes and States in the Post-Hegemonic Era*, ed. Philip G. Cerny (Aldershot: Edward Elgar Publishing Limited, 1993), pp. 3–19; Jeff Worsham, *Other People's Money: Policy Change, Congress, And Bank Regulation* (Boulder, C.O.: Westview Press, 1997); Sassen, "Global Financial Centers"; Sassen, *Cities in a World Economy*; Thomas Oatley *et al.*, "The Political Economy of Global Finance: A Network Model", *Perspectives on Politics* 11, No. 1 (2013): 133–53; Woo, *Business and Politics in Asia's Key Financial Centres — Hong Kong, Singapore and Shanghai*.
5. Mark Yeandle, "Global Financial Centres Index 18" (London, U.K.: Z/Yen Group and Qatar Financial Centre Authority, September 2015); Mark Yeandle, "Global Financial Centres Index 17" (London, U.K.: Z/Yen Group and Qatar Financial Centre Authority, March 2015); Dennis Brandes *et al.*, "Deloitte Global Wealth Management Centre Ranking 2015" (Zurich, Switzerland: Deloitte Consulting AG, 2015).
6. Saskia Sassen, "Whose City Is It? Globalization and the Formation of New Claims," *Public Culture* 8, No. 2 (1996): 205–23; Joseph E. Stiglitz, *Globalization and Its Discontents* (New York: W.W. Norton, 2003).
7. Eduardo Levy Yeyati and Tomas Williams, Financial Globalization in Emerging Economies: Much Ado about Nothing?, *Policy Research Working Papers* (Washington, D.C.: The World Bank, 2011), http://elibrary.worldbank.org/doi/abs/10.1596/1813-9450-5624.
8. Eswar Prasad *et al.*, "Effects of Financial Globalization on Developing Countries: Some Empirical Evidence" (Washington, D.C.: International Monetary Fund, March 17, 2003); Sergio L. Schmukler, "Benefits and Risks of Financial Globalization: Challenges for Developing Countries" (Washington, D.C.: World Bank, June 2004); M. Ayhan Kose *et al.*, "Financial Globalization and Economic Policies," Discussion Paper Series (Bonn, Germany: Institute for the Study of Labor, February 2009).

9. Robert G. King and Ross Levine, "Finance and Growth: Schumpeter Might Be Right," *The Quarterly Journal of Economics* 108, No. 3 (August 1, 1993): 717–37; Thorsten Beck, Ross Levine, and Norman Loayza, "Finance and the Sources of Growth," *Journal of Financial Economics* 58, No. 1–2 (2000): 261–300; Asli Demirguc-Kunt and Ross Levine, "Finance, Financial Sector Policies, And Long-Run Growth," *Research Working Papers* 1, No. 1 (2008): 1–82.
10. Sassen, *Cities in a World Economy*; John Friedman, "The World City Hypothesis," in The City: The City in Global Context, ed. Michael Pacione (London: Routledge, 2002), pp. 151–63.
11. S. Rajaratnam, "'Global City' Success for Spore: Raja," *The Straits Times*, February 7, 1972.
12. Gerald A. Epstein, *Financialization and the World Economy* (Cheltenham, UK: Edward Elgar Publishing, 2005), p. 3.
13. Greta R. Krippner, "The Financialization of the American Economy," *Socio-Economic Review* 3, No. 2 (May 1, 2005): 173–208; Sarah Hall, "Geographies of Money and Finance II: Financialization and Financial Subjects," *Progress in Human Geography* 36, No. 3 (2012): 403–11; Mark Kear, "Governing Homo Subprimicus: Beyond Financial Citizenship, Exclusion, and Rights," *Antipode* 45, No. 4 (September 1, 2013): 926–46; Lai and Tan, "'Neighbours First, Bankers Second.'"
14. Wei Han Wong, "Singapore's Asset Management Industry Grew Strongly in 2014: MAS," The Straits Times, July 21, 2015, http://www.straitstimes.com/business/economy/singapores-asset-management-industry-grew-strongly-in-2014-mas; Nicole Tan, "Singapore Economy Grew 2.1% in 2015, Beating Expectations," Channel NewsAsia, January 4, 2016, sec. Business, http://www.channelnewsasia.com/news/business/singapore-economy-grew-2/2396126.html.
15. Department of Statistics Singapore, "Share of GDP by Industry," February 17, 2015, http://www.singstat.gov.sg/statistics/visualising-data/charts/share-of-gdp-by-industry.
16. Manuel F. Montes, "Tokyo, Hong Kong and Singapore as Competing Financial Centres," *Journal of Asian Business* 18, No. 1 (1999): 153–68.
17. Ian Patrick Austin, *Goh Keng Swee And Southeast Asian Governance* (Singapore: Marshall Cavendish Academic, 2004).
18. Sassen, *Cities in a World Economy*.
19. E.P. Davis, "International Financial Centres — An Industrial Analysis," *Bank of England Discussion Paper*, (September 1990); Thomas Gehrig, "Cities and the Geography of Financial Centers," in *Economies of Cities: Theoretical Perspectives*, ed. Jean-Marie Huriot and Jacques-Francois Thiesse (Cambridge: Cambridge University Press, 2000), pp. 415–46.
20. Linda Low, *The Political Economy of a City-State Revised* (Singapore: Marshall Cavendish, 2006); Linda Y. C. Lim, "Fifty Years of Development in the Singapore Economy: An Introductory Review," *The Singapore Economic Review* 60, No. 3 (August 1, 2015): 1502002, doi:10.1142/S0217590815020026.

BUT ONCE YOU SEE SINGAPORE AS A GLOBAL CITY, THE PROBLEM OF HINTERLAND BECOMES UNIMPORTANT BECAUSE FOR A GLOBAL CITY, THE WORLD IS ITS HINTERLAND.

S. RAJARATNAM
ADDRESS TO THE SINGAPORE PRESS CLUB
6 FEBRUARY 1972

CHAPTER TWO

Global Cities in a Global Economy

As hubs of global financial activity, global financial centres are invariably situated within highly interconnected global cities. Indeed, the latest iteration of the Global Financial Centres Index (GFCI) shows that the vast majority of the world's most competitive financial centres are situated within major global cities.[1] Singapore is currently ranked third on the GFCI, lagging behind only London and New York, who are placed first and second respectively.

In all cases, financial activity both hinges upon the central position of these cities in the global economy and continues to sustain their economic viability. While this tendency towards centralisation in the urban city centre is discussed at greater length in Chapter 4, it suffices to say that global financial centres have benefitted immensely from their central positions within a rapidly globalising economy.

Furthermore, there is a strong spatial element to these sociopolitical impacts of globalisation. For instance, globalisation has been described as the "re-territorialisation of both socioeconomic and political–institutional spaces that unfolds simultaneously upon multiple, superimposed geographical scales".[2] This 're-territorialisation' has resulted in the emergence of global cities as 'command centres' of the global economy.[3]

Indeed, the rise of today's leading global cities coincides with the rapid globalization that has marked the 1990s and 2000s.[4] However, Singapore's experience with globalisation far precedes this period. The city-state has from its independence perceived itself as a global city that, despite its lack of a natural hinterland, can nonetheless tap on the rest of the world as its hinterland and hence derive its economic prospects from the global economy.[5]

As the following sections will show, it is this early recognition of the economic benefits of globalisation that has allowed Singapore to 'leapfrog' its neighbours in economic development and establish itself as Southeast Asia's key financial centre and leading global city. The economic forces that have propelled globalisation in Singapore are discussed next.

Economic Forces

There is little doubt that globalisation is first and foremost an economically driven phenomenon. Indeed, one could even go so far as to suggest that globalisation is neither an entirely new nor novel phenomenon. Indeed, international trade has existed for almost as long as civilisations have existed. From ancient Greece to Han Dynasty China to renaissance Europe, nation-states have long been engaged in the cross-border trade of goods and services. However, it was only in the early 19th century that forces of globalisation were capable of influencing domestic prices and living standards.[6]

The establishment of Bretton Woods institutions such as the World Bank, International Monetary Fund (IMF), and what would later become the World Trade Organisation (WTO) after the Second World War would serve to further accelerate economic globalisation by facilitating trade liberalisation, establishing an international payment system, and providing support for economic development.[7] The WTO's 'most favoured nation' (MFN) treatment was particularly instrumental in driving global trade, by ensuring that WTO members extend to each other the same trading terms that they would provide to their 'most favoured' partners.

Given that international trade had already existed in antiquity, there is a need to establish a clear definition and understanding of 'globalisation'. This will help ensure clarity in the discussions that will follow. While the phenomenon of states trading with each other in a global market place long precedes the current discourse on economic globalisation, the understanding of globalisation that is used in this book is predicated upon its impact on a city's domestic economic activity and quality of living.

Furthermore, and as I will discuss later in this chapter, the accelerated pace of globalisation that was experienced in the 1990s and 2000s occurred as a consequence of advancements in information and communications technology (ICT) and a similarly technologically-driven reduction in transportation and travel costs. Globalisation, understood in this context, is therefore strongly associated with, and even identifiable by, its positive impacts on the socioeconomic well-being of a country as well as the facilitative role of technological advancements.

Regardless, international trade is a phenomenon that Singapore has long been familiar with. It has been noted that the origins of economic globalisation in Singapore can be traced back to 1819, which was the year that the British colonial government designated Singapore a free port, establishing the island as a key node in global maritime trade.[8] Singapore's strategic geographical location has since been the linchpin for its successful development as a global financial centre and global city.

Indeed, the success of Singapore's financial sector has always hinged upon its position as a global trading hub as well as the growing presence of MNCs and other 'advanced producer services' in its city centre.[9] While growing trade activity had driven a need for related-financial services such as shipping and maritime insurance, the growing presence of advanced producer services, such as accountancy and legal firms, served to sustain a thriving financial sector ecosystem.

As Singapore's economy became increasingly globalised, beginning in the 1970s through the 2000s, its stature and position as a global financial centre rose in tandem. As discussed in the next chapter, this close interrelation between economic globalisation and financial is driven by an increasingly complex economy's need for new financial instruments that could serve to reallocate capital and resources more efficiently.

Just how globalised is Singapore's economy exactly? According to the KOF Index of Globalization 2016 that was compiled by ETH, Singapore is ranked first in the world for Economic Globalization, and sixth in the overall Globalization Index, which includes measures of actual economic flows, economic restrictions, information flows, personal contact, and cultural proximity.[10] This makes Singapore one of the most globalised economies in the world. This is also reflected in Singapore's economic data.

As of 2015, Singapore's exports of goods and services as percentage of its GDP stand at 176.5%.[11] This figure was 123% in 1965, when Singapore had first gained independence, reflecting a marked increase and correspondingly, significant globalisation of Singapore's economy. However, this figure has also fluctuated over the years. Table 2.1 provides several datapoints of Singapore's exports of goods and services as percentage of its GDP over the past two decades.

As Table 2.1 shows, Singapore's exports of goods and services as percentage of GDP has fluctuated in tandem with the state of the regional and global economy. For instance, Singapore enjoyed strong exports in the years 1995, 2000, and 2006. However, exports dipped markedly in 1998 and 2009.

Table 2.1: Singapore's Exports of Goods and Services as Percentage of GDP

	1995	1998	2000	2006	2009	2015
Exports of Goods and Services (% of GDP)	181	168	189	230	192	176

Adapted from World Bank (2016), Exports of Goods and Services (% of GDP)[12]

These figures reflect impacts of the 1997 Asian Financial Crisis (AFC) and the 2008 Global Financial Crisis (GFC), as global demand contracted in the aftermath of the two crises.

The relatively low figure of 176% in 2015 also reflects continued global economic weakness, as the United States and the EU struggle to recover from the impacts of the GFC, and China faces an impending economic slowdown. A similar trend can be found in Table 2.2, which shows Singapore's net inflow of foreign direct investment (FDI) as percentage of GDP, although in this case, there was a significant uptick in net FDI inflow in 2015.

As the trends exhibited in Tables 2.1 and 2.2 show, Singapore's economy is highly dependent on the state of the global and regional economy. In particular, external shocks such as financial crises can result in significant declines in both exports and inward FDI. This interdependency between Singapore's domestic economy and global economic events suggests a significant extent of economic globalisation.

While this interdependency has made Singapore's domestic economy more vulnerable to external shocks and perturbations, the rapid globalisation of Singapore's economy has nonetheless

Table 2.2: Singapore's Net FDI Inflow as Percentage of GDP

	1995	1998	2000	2006	2009	2015
Foreign Direct Investment, Net Inflows (% of GDP)	13.1	8.53	16.2	25	12.4	22.3

Adapted from World Bank (2016), Foreign Direct Investment, Net Inflow (% of GDP)[13]

Table 2.3: Singapore's GDP and GDP per capita

	1965	1995	1998	2000	2006	2009	2015
GDP (Current USD)	974 million	87.89 billion	85.708 billion	95.834 billion	147.797 billion	192.408 billion	292.739 billion
GDP per capita (Current USD)	516	24,937	21,824	23,792	33,580	38,578	52,889

Adapted from World Bank (2016), GDP per capita (current US$) and World Bank (2016), *GDP (current US$)*[14]

brought forth substantial economic gains. Table 2.3 shows Singapore's GDP and GDP per capita figures in current US Dollars. As both measures show, Singapore's economy has grown exponentially over the years. This is in large part due to the significant exports and inflows of capital that have accompanied Singapore's rapid economic globalisation.

These figures stand in stark contrast to Singapore's GDP of US$974 million and GDP per capita of US$516 in 1965, when it had first attained independence. Given its lack of a hinterland and the limited scale of its geographical size and labour force, these vast improvements in Singapore's GDP and GDP per capita can almost entirely be attributed to the rapid globalisation of its economy and, as the next section will discuss, the government's ability to identify and capitalise on the various opportunities that have emerged from globalisation. Indeed, Singapore has often seen economic globalisation as its only option, having lost its natural hinterland upon separation from Malaysia.

As this section has shown, Singapore has benefited immensely from the economic forces of globalisation that have placed it at the centre of global trade flows. However, economic globalisation is not merely a passive process that has simply 'happened' to Singapore. Rather, Singapore's approach towards harnessing the economic gains of globalisation is the result of deliberate policy and political action, enacted in response to Singapore's geostrategic vulnerabilities. In particular, Singapore's relatively small size and its lack of a natural hinterland have required it to seek out economic opportunities outside its borders.

It has also been noted that the most globalised economies tend to be small states that rely on economic openness to acquire the goods and services that cannot be produced domestically as well as gain access to larger markets for its firms and industries.[15] The impetus for economic globalisation is therefore particularly high for small states such as Singapore, with the consequence being concerted efforts by policymakers and political leaders to actively globalise their markets. However, there are also sociopolitical implications of Singapore's rapid economic globalisation. These sociopolitical drivers and implications of globalisation are discussed next.

Sociopolitical Drivers

While economic imperatives have often driven processes of globalisation, there are also significant sociopolitical implications of globalisation. However, the sociopolitical implications of globalisation are far more complex. Specifically, globalisation has sharpened distinctions between the political left and right, on the one hand emphasising global governance and the need for greater state interventions to address policy problems, and on the other, economic liberalisation and a 'retreat of the state' in the belief that markets need to be free of state interventions and distortions in order to function efficiently.[16]

It is also important to note that the prevalence of either of these two narratives — 'retreat of the state' versus greater state intervention — were as much driven by circumstances as they were by the conscious choice of states. While the globalisation narrative of the 2000s had downplayed the role of the state and emphasised instead a neoliberal approach to governance that grants greater autonomy to the private sector, the onset of the GFC had resulted in a shift in public discourse back towards the need for government interventions in preventing future crises.[17]

Given this context, the development of Singapore's governance and public administration system bears the imprint of both neoliberalism and state interventionism. Long held up as a proponent of what is known as the "Developmental State Model", Singapore has, since its independence, relied on extensive state intervention and the role of 'lead agencies', such as the Economic Development Board (EDB) in the development of its economy.[18] Such tendencies towards 'developmentalism' and state interventions have also often extended into non-economic realms of policy.[19]

This has been achieved through the proliferation of state agencies, such as semi-autonomous statutory boards and government-linked companies (GLCs), that are all involved in the delivery of public services, albeit through different organisational forms and policy pathways.[20] In particular, statutory boards represent 'lead agencies' within their domains, providing the necessary expertise and organisational leadership for policymaking within that domain. However, the semi-autonomous nature of these statutory boards, as well as the government's foray into private sector-styled organisation in the form of GLCs, alludes to a simultaneous tendency towards neoliberalism.

This is particularly the case in Singapore's public administration and bureaucracy. For instance, the government has sought to incorporate private sector-styled management practices into its various public agencies. Known as 'New Public Management', this incorporation of private sector management into Singapore's public sector includes delegation of more managerial autonomy to statutory boards, introduction of market-based measures of performance and budgeting in public agencies, and the contracting out of certain services and functions to private companies.[21]

However, it should be noted that this spread of New Public Management and other neoliberal principles or practices of governance does not equate to a decline in state strength or capacity. Rather, these reforms are often seen as strategic government decisions aimed at enhancing bureaucratic efficiency and responsiveness, with the efficacy of these reforms itself dependent upon the strength and capacity of the Singaporean state.[22] Hence, while liberalisation has occurred in the realm of public administration, political governance in Singapore remains centred on its ruling People's Action Party (PAP).

What has emerged is a strong developmental state that is at the same time able to incorporate private sector efficiency into its public service delivery processes. Indeed, both these processes — adherence to the developmental state model and new public management reforms — are predicated upon a need to ensure economic growth and bureaucratic efficiency, both of which are often seen as precursors to national economic competitiveness amid an increasingly globalised economy.

Aside from such domestic politico-administrative concerns, economic globalisation has also prompted important shifts to Singapore's approach towards engaging with the region and the global economy at large. For instance, the policy scholar M Ramesh has noted how the Singaporean state has managed to internalise and foster economic globalisation in its domestic policy processes, in the process expanding both state resources and policy choices.[23]

In other words, the Singapore government has embraced globalisation and sought to turn what is often seen as a limiting factor into a national advantage. An oft-cited example is the government's early efforts at encouraging multinational companies (MNCs) to establish their regional headquarters within the city-state, at a time when many other Southeast Asian states were seeking to protect their domestic companies from these MNCs. This strategy has resulted in large inflows of investments as well as technology transfers, effectively establishing Singapore's position as a global business hub.

A reverse, but no less important, process is found in the government's subsequent 'regionalisation policy', through which domestic firms were encouraged to establish operations in the region.[24] Part of this strategy has involved the establishing of Singapore-developed or jointly developed industrial parks in other Asian countries, and encouraging Singaporean firms to locate parts, if not all, of their production processes within these parks.[25] These two strategies — transnationalisation and regionalisation — represent Singapore's efforts at growing its domestic economy through deeper engagements with the regional and global economy.

Associated with these efforts are the government's parallel efforts at establishing closer diplomatic relations with key economic partners such as the US, China, and its Southeast Asian neighbours. With regards to Southeast Asia, Singapore has always been a strong supporter of the Association of South

East Nations (ASEAN), having been a founding member of the Association and remaining a strong proponent of ASEAN diplomatic processes. Indeed, Singapore's support for ASEAN serves to provide it with a regional economic hinterland that its firms and businesses can easily access.

As such, it is clear that the Singapore government sees globalisation not as a threat, but a strategic advantage to be harnessed for encouraging economic growth and development. Indeed, Singapore's approach towards engaging forces of globalisation drives both its economic regional strategy and its diplomatic relations with other nations. A recent example of this is the formation of the Global Governance Group (3G), under the G20 framework. Along with its earlier efforts at founding the Forum of Small States (FOSS), Singapore has frequently leveraged upon such institutions to engage with global politics.

In short, sociopolitical considerations have often driven Singapore's approach of engaging with, and even incorporating, forces of globalisation into its policy processes, for the express purposes of ensuring continued economic growth and protecting its sovereign interests. Sociopolitical drivers and implications of globalisation in Singapore therefore exist at the domestic, regional, and international levels of governance.

However, this state-driven approach to globalisation has not come without challenges. In particular, Singapore's approach of recruiting foreign talent to supplement its ageing population has led to sociopolitical backlash arising from strains to its public infrastructure as well as growing inequality.[26] This is compounded by ongoing difficulties with economic structuring and raising productivity. One way that the government has sought to address these challenges is through technology.

Technology

While economic forces have long driven global trade and economic relations, the accelerated pace of globalisation that occurred during the 1990s and 2000s was largely facilitated by the role of technology. Two types of technology have been particularly instrumental in driving globalisation: transportation and ICT. Advancements in mass transportation and ICT have served to compress space and time, reducing the effort and resources required to transport people, goods, and capital across national boundaries.

The impacts of mass transportation on global trade and travel are well-known. For instance, the advent of container shipping has allowed firms to transport large quantities of goods more efficiently and economically. As a consequence, major maritime cities have emerged to act as conduits and control centres of global trade.[27] Container shipping remains the most economically efficient and hence popular mode of transport for goods, with container ships continuing to expand in capacity.[28]

However, it is only with the introduction of air travel that the movement of people across borders could be made more efficient. Indeed, the emergence of affordable commercial air travel has resulted in exponential growth in global tourism. More importantly, it has shorted geographical distances by making it faster and easier to travel across the world. Like container shipping, there have also been marked increases in the physical sizes of commercial aircraft, as airlines seek to expand their passenger capacity.

Aside from commercial airlines, airfreight has also emerged as a fast, albeit more costly, means of transporting goods across countries. In both cases, container shipping and commercial air travel has facilitated the efficient and rapid transport of goods and people across national boundaries. This has in turn contributed towards global trade volumes and human capital mobility. However, the impact of mass transportation as a catalyst of globalisation pales in comparison to that of ICT.

Indeed, ICT has contributed immensely to economic globalisation over the past two decades. In particular, it has been noted that advanced information technologies allow nations to "sustain deeper levels of economic integration with one another".[29] This is particularly the case for finance, with US$1.5 trillion moved around the world every day.[30] While early telecommunications technologies such as the telephone or fax have allowed for instantaneous communication across spatial boundaries, it was only with the emergence of the internet that ICT took on a central role in driving globalisation.

Originally developed by the US military as a secure computer network, the internet is fundamentally a framework that brings together all forms of electronic media — whether telephony, video, or data — into one delivery mechanism.[31] With the internet, information and data can be rapidly moved across geographical boundaries. The possibilities of the internet are far too wide and multitudinous to discuss in the span of this chapter. A few key examples will have to suffice.

The most significant impact of the internet on global trade is arguably e-commerce. With e-commerce platforms, consumers are now able to purchase goods and products directly from retailers all over the world, bypassing brick-and-mortar shops. For e-retailers, this eliminates key business costs such as rental or wages. As of 2015, Singapore's e-commerce market has been valued at US$1 billion; it is expected to be worth US$5.4 billion by 2025.[32] Indeed, Singapore is well-known as an early adopter of new and emerging technologies. It also boasts an extraordinarily high level of technological diffusion, despite the small size of its population.

For instance, Singapore's mobile phone penetration as of 2015 is 148.4% while its household residential wired broadband penetration rate for 2016 is 101.9%.[33] In other words, there are almost 50% more mobile phones than there are people in Singapore. Such high rates of internet adoption have been beneficial for businesses, especially those that have been able to leverage upon e-commerce and business-to-business (B2B) platforms to expand their consumer market base, reduce costs of production, and raise labour productivity.[34]

For firms, such advancements in ICT have allowed for the disaggregation of production chains across national boundaries, with firms now able to locate different components of the production chain in different geographical locations, as they seek out the most cost effective locations to perform these functions. Given Singapore's limited geographical space and small market, such disaggregation of the production chain has been particularly crucial for Singaporean firms.

This has in particular included the location of Singaporean businesses in cities that have established close diplomatic and business ties with the Singapore government. These include the Suzhou Industrial Park, Tianjin Eco-City, and the Chongqing Connectivity Initiative (CCI). All three instances are government-to-government projects that allow Singaporean firms to access a larger market while at the same time contribute to infrastructural and market development in these Chinese cities.

It is through the availability of advanced ICT tools that firms are able to operate across national boundaries in such a manner. The reverse is also true, with regards to Singapore's position as Asia's top logistics hub.[35] Given Singapore's global connectivity, its sociopolitical stability as well as the availability of world-class infrastructure and a skilled labour pool, Singapore has become a prime location for firms to locate part of their supply chains, especially in the aerospace, petrochemicals, electronics, healthcare, and pharmaceuticals industries.[36]

There has therefore been a dual movement when it comes to the impact of technology on the disaggregation of global supply chains. On the one hand, Singaporean firms are now able to relocate certain parts of their supply chain in other countries, especially those aspects that require great cost effectiveness, especially in terms of labour costs. On the other hand, Singapore has also benefited from the influx of foreign firms that have chosen to locate parts of their supply chains in the city-state. These firms have provided both investments and jobs for the domestic workforce.

This corresponds to the Singapore government's strategies of regionalisation and transnationalisation, which were both discussed in the previous section. While the ability of Singapore's domestic firms to establish a presence in regional economies now rely heavily on the ability of these firms to leverage on ICT to coordinate their cross-border operations, Singapore's attractiveness to MNCs seeking to establish their regional and even international headquarters in the city-state hinges upon the availability of ICT and other technological infrastructure.

This latter need to ensure the availability of reliable IT and ICT infrastructure is particularly relevant to Singapore's financial services sector, with the government's efforts at developing new financial districts, such as the Marina Bay Financial Centre (MBFC) and Changi Business Park, involving 'spatial enhancements' in the form of physical and digital infrastructure.[37] This is especially significant for Changi Business Park, which houses many of the IT and data centres of major financial institutions.[38]

At the individual level, the internet (along with other ICT platforms) have brought an unprecedented level of connectivity and global exposure. Aside from retail, individuals now have access to the online delivery of content. This is particularly the case with Massive Open Online Courses (MOOCs), which are online educational courses typically provided by accredited universities and which award participants with a certification upon completion of the course.

This exposure to the internet, along with Singapore's strengths in education and talent management, has resulted in the formation of a highly skilled and IT-savvy workforce. This has in turn made Singapore highly attractive to banks and financial institutions, since they are able to staff their operations in Singapore with a locally available skilled workforce capable of handling the various specialised functions associated with banking and finance.[39]

Financial Globalisation: Confluence of Economics, Politics and Technology

As this chapter has shown, globalisation has wide-ranging implications for Singapore. As an economic phenomenon, globalisation has brought forth significant economic gains and opportunities. This has in turn required active effort on the part of the government in leveraging on these opportunities, even as it grapples with the various sociopolitical challenges that have emerged with globalisation. This has been greatly aided by advanced ICT platforms, which have catalysed economic globalisation and, at the same time, provided the tools necessary for global city-states to thrive in the global political economy.

As nexuses of global capital flows, the existence and continued success of global financial centres such as Singapore depend heavily on economic globalisation. Indeed, economic globalisation is strongly related to a similar process of financial globalisation, which has served to further stimulate wide-scale liberalisation and economic integration in the world's major financial centres.[40] As is the case with economic globalisation, financial globalisation involves a confluence of economics, politics, and technology.[41]

It has, for instance, been noted that financial globalisation contributes immensely to economic development,[42] even as it gives rise to new sociopolitical configurations of 'governing elites'.[43] In the case of Singapore, policymakers and industry actors have often worked in tandem to 'co-create' financial policies that have been instrumental in ensuring financial sector growth and market stability.[44]

Furthermore, the emergence and spread of new financial technologies, or 'FinTech', raised the potential of new growth areas and opportunities,[45] even as they bring forth new regulatory challenges[46]. In view of these, Singapore is seeking to transform itself into a 'smart financial centre' that is capable of both leveraging on the economic opportunities emerging from FinTech and addressing the risks involved.[47] The ways in which finance has impacted Singapore's economy, sociopolitical context and technological developments is the topic of the next chapter.

Endnotes

1. Mark Yeandle, "Global Financial Centre Index 19" (London, U.K.: Z/Yen Group and Qatar Financial Centre Authority, March 2016).
2. Neil Brenner, "Globalisation as Reterritorialisation: The Re-Scaling of Urban Governance in the European Union," *Urban Studies* 36, No. 3 (March 1, 1999): 431–451, doi:10.1080/0042098993466.

3. Saskia J. Sassen, *Cities in a World Economy*, 4th ed. (California: SAGE Publications, Inc., 2011).
4. Joseph E. Stiglitz, *Globalization and Its Discontents* (New York: W.W. Norton, 2003).
5. S. Rajaratnam, "'Global City' Success for S'pore: Raja," *The Straits Times*, February 7, 1972.
6. Kevin H. O'Rourke and Jeffrey G. Williamson, "When Did Globalisation Begin?" *European Review of Economic History* 6, No. 1 (April 1, 2002): 23–50, doi:10.1017/S1361491602000023.
7. Neil Warren, "Internet and Globalisation," in *Economics of Globalisation*, ed. Partha Gangopadhyay and Manas Chatterji (Aldershot: Ashgate Publishing, Ltd., 2005), pp. 192–193.
8. M. Ramesh, "Economic Globalization and Policy Choices," *Governance: An International Journal of Policy and Administration* 8, No. 2 (1995): 246.
9. Sassen, *Cities in a World Economy*; J. J. Woo, *Business and Politics in Asia's Key Financial Centres — Hong Kong, Singapore and Shanghai*, 1st ed. (Singapore: Springer, 2016); J. J. Woo, *Singapore as an International Financial Centre: History, Politics and Policy* (London: Palgrave Macmillan, 2016).
10. ETH, "KOF Index of Globalization 2016," KOF Index of Globalization (Zurich, Switzerland: ETH, 2016).
11. World Bank, "Exports of Goods and Services (% of GDP)" (Washington, D.C.: World Bank, 2016).
12. *Ibid.*
13. World Bank, "Foreign Direct Investment, Net Inflows (% of GDP) | Data," *World Bank Database*, 2016, http://data.worldbank.org/indicator/BX.KLT.DINV.WD.GD.ZS?locations=SG&view=chart.
14. World Bank, "GDP per Capita (Current USS)," *World Bank Database*, 2016, http://data.worldbank.org/indicator/NY.GDP.PCAP.CD?locations=SG&view=chart; World Bank, "GDP (Current US$) | Data," *World Bank Database*, accessed September 23, 2016, http://data.worldbank.org/indicator/NY.GDP.MKTP.CD?locations=SG&view=chart.
15. Katherine Yester, "Measuring Globalization," *Foreign Policy*, November 20, 2009, https://foreignpolicy.com/2009/11/20/measuring-globalization/.
16. James Putzel, "Globalization, Liberalization, and Prospects for the State," *International Political Science Review* 26, No. 1 (January 1, 2005): 5–16, doi:10.1177/0192512105047893; Susan Strange, *The Retreat of the State: The Diffusion of Power in the World Economy* (Cambridge: Cambridge University Press, 1996); A. Claire Cutler, Virginia Haufler, and Tony Porter, *Private Authority and International Affairs* (Albany: State University of New York Press, 1999).
17. Michael Howlett and Raul P. Lejano, "Tales From the Crypt The Rise and Fall (and Rebirth?) Of Policy Design," *Administration & Society* 45, No. 3 (April 1, 2013): 357–381.
18. W. G. Huff, "The Developmental State, Government, and Singapore's Economic Development since 1960," *World Development* 23, No. 8 (August 1995): 1421–1438; Linda Low, "The Singapore Developmental State in the New Economy and Polity," *The Pacific Review* 14, No. 3 (January 1, 2001): 411–441.

19. James Lee, "Developmentalism, Social Welfare and State Capacity in East Asia: Integrating Housing and Social Security in Singapore," *Journal of Asian Public Policy* 2, No. 2 (2009): 157–170, doi:10.1080/17516230903027880.
20. J.J. Woo, "Singapore's Policy Style: Statutory Boards as Policymaking Units," *Journal of Asian Public Policy* 8, No. 2 (2014): 120–133.
21. M. Shamsul Haque, "Structures of New Public Management in Malaysia and Singapore: Alternative Views," *The Journal of Comparative Asian Development* 1, No. 1 (2002): 71–86; M. Shamsul Haque, "Governance and Bureaucracy in Singapore: Contemporary Reforms and Implications," *International Political Science Review* 25, No. 2 (April 1, 2004): 227–240; Eliza W. Y. Lee and M. Shamsul Haque, "The New Public Management Reform and Governance in Asian NICs: A Comparison of Hong Kong and Singapore," *Governance* 19, No. 4 (2006): 605–626.
22. Lee and Haque, *The New Public Management Reform and Governance in Asian NICs.*
23. M. Ramesh, *Economic Globalization and Policy Choices.*
24. Henry Wai-Chung Yeung, "State Intervention and Neoliberalism in the Globalizing World Economy: Lessons from Singapore's Regionalization Programme," *The Pacific Review* 13, No. 1 (January 1, 2000): 133–162, doi:10.1080/095127400363677.
25. Alexius Pereira, "Singapore's Regionalization Strategy," *Journal of the Asia Pacific Economy* 10, No. 3 (January 1, 2005): 380–396, doi:10.1080/13547860500163480.
26. Linda Low, "Globalisation and the Political Economy of Singapore's Policy on Foreign Talent and High Skills," *Journal of Education and Work* 15, No. 4 (December 1, 2002): 409–425, doi:10.1080/1363908022000023551; Kenneth Paul Tan, "Singapore in 2011: A 'New Normal' in Politics?" *Asian Survey* 52, No. 1 (February 2012): 220–226; Derek Da Cunha, *Breakthrough: Roadmap for Singapore's Political Future* (Singapore: Straits Times Press Reference, 2012).
27. Ann Verhetsel and Steve Sel, "World Maritime Cities: From Which Cities Do Container Shipping Companies Make Decisions?" *Transport Policy*, SI: TBGS The International Forum on Shipping, Ports and Airports (IFSPA) 2008, 16, No. 5 (September 2009): 240–250, doi:10.1016/j.tranpol.2009.08.002.
28. Ben Ames, "Post-Panamax Containerships Reach East Coast Ports — DC Velocity," *DC Velocity*, July 14, 2016, http://www.dcvelocity.com/articles/20160714-post-panamax-containerships-reach-east-coast-ports/.
29. Yester, *Measuring Globalization.*
30. *Ibid.*
31. Warren, *Internet and Globalisation*, p. 194.
32. Channel NewsAsia, "Singapore E-Commerce Market to Exceed S$7b in 2025: Report," *Channel News Asia*, May 24, 2016, http://www.channelnewsasia.com/news/business/singapore-e-commerce/2811118.html.
33. Infocomm Development Authority of Singapore, "Telecommunications," *Infocomm Development Authority of Singapore Website*, 2016, https://www.ida.gov.sg/Tech-Scene-News/Facts-and-Figures/Telecommunications.
34. Warren, *Internet and Globalisation*, p. 199.

35. Economic Development Board, "Industries — Logistics and Supply Chain Management," *Singapore Economic Development Board — Investing Business in Singapore*, October 2, 2015,/content/edb/en/industries/industries/logistics-and-supply-chain-management.html.
36. *Ibid.*
37. Woo, *Singapore as an International Financial Centre: History, Politics and Policy*, pp. 48–49.
38. Karen P.Y. Lai, "Singapore's Economic Landscapes: Local Transformations and Global Networks," in *Changing Landscapes of Singapore: Old Tensions, New Discoveries*, ed. Elaine Lynn-Ee Ho, Yuan Woon Chih, and Kamalini Ramdas (Singapore: NUS Press, 2013), p. 210.
39. Jun Jie Woo, "Three 'T's behind Singapore's Future as a Leading Financial Centre," *TODAY*, June 26, 2014, http://www.todayonline.com/business/three-ts-behind-singapores-future-leading-financial-centre.
40. Eswar Prasad *et al.*, "Effects of Financial Globalization on Developing Countries: Some Empirical Evidence" (Washington, D.C.: International Monetary Fund, March 17, 2003); M. Ayhan Kose *et al.*, "Financial Globalization and Economic Policies," Discussion Paper Series (Bonn, Germany: Institute for the Study of Labor, February 2009).
41. Philip G. Cerny, "The Dynamics of Financial Globalization: Technology, Market Structure, and Policy Response," *Policy Sciences* 27, No. 4 (1994): 319–342, doi:10.1007/BF01000063; Woo, "Three 'T's behind Singapore's Future as a Leading Financial Centre"; Woo, *Business and Politics in Asia's Key Financial Centres — Hong Kong, Singapore and Shanghai*.
42. Jith Jayaratne and Philip E. Strahan, "The Finance-Growth Nexus: Evidence from Bank Branch Deregulation," *The Quarterly Journal of Economics* 111, No. 3 (August 1, 1996): 639–670; Xiaoyan Zhang and Dafei Chen, "The Influence of Financial Industry Cluster on Economic Growth: Three Economic Zones in China," *Accounting and Finance Research* 2, No. 4 (October 13, 2013), doi:10.5430/afr.v2n4p69.
43. Natasha Hamilton-Hart, *Asian States, Asian Bankers: Central Banking in Southeast Asia* (New York: Cornell University Press, 2002).
44. J. J. Woo, "Policy Relations and Policy Subsystems: Financial Policy in Hong Kong and Singapore," *International Journal of Public Administration* 38, No. 8 (2015): 553–561; Woo, *Singapore as an International Financial Centre: History, Politics and Policy*.
45. J. J. Woo, *Three 'T's behind Singapore's Future as a Leading Financial Centre*.
46. Sharon Chen and Chanyaporn Chanjaroen, "Singapore to Regulate Fintech Firms Only When They Pose Risk," *Bloomberg*, April 13, 2016, http://www.bloomberg.com/news/articles/2016-04-13/singapore-to-regulate-fintech-firms-only-when-they-pose-risks.
47. Ravi Menon, "A Smart Financial Centre" (Keynote Address, Global Technology Law Conference 2015, Singapore, June 29, 2015), http://www.mas.gov.sg/news-and-publications/speeches-and-monetary-policy-statements/speeches/2015/a-smart-financial-centre.aspx.

NEOLIBERALIZATION HAS MEANT, IN SHORT, THE FINANCIALIZATION OF EVERYTHING. THERE WAS UNQUESTIONABLY A POWER SHIFT AWAY FROM PRODUCTION TO THE WORLD OF FINANCE.

DAVID HARVEY
A BRIEF HISTORY OF NEOLIBERALISM

CHAPTER THREE

The Prevalence of Finance

As economies become increasingly globalised, interdependent, and integrated with each other, there has emerged a need for cross-border payments systems as well as other forms of financial services such as shipping insurance or maritime finance that could support regional and global trade in goods and services. This prompted the emergence of banks, insurers, and other financial institutions in many major port cities to satisfy the demand for financial services and insurance among shippers and other shipping logistics providers.

In fact, physical traces of this strong linkage between trade and finance can still be found in Singapore's urban form. For instance, Singapore's Central Business District (CBD) was established in close proximity to the Singapore River (where warehouses used to be located and barges loaded with goods used to ply) as well as the Keppel Shipyard. This close proximity allowed financiers easy access to their clientele in the shipping industry.

However, the financial services sector has since emerged as a growth industry in its own right, currently contributing to 12.6% of Singapore's GDP.[1] It is expected to remain a key driver of economic growth in Singapore for the foreseeable future, especially in light of an ongoing contraction of Singapore's manufacturing industry. This has given financial institutions significant clout and influence within Singapore's sociopolitical landscape, especially in terms of their ability to influence or participate in the government's financial policy processes.[2]

Furthermore, finance and technology have often intersected, giving rise to what is known as financial technology, or FinTech, which involves the utilisation of big data and analytics tools to develop new financial instruments and derive new sources of growth and value. The emergence of FinTech has therefore brought forth new opportunities for financial sector development, even as it comes with new regulatory challenges. Like globalisation, there are profound economic, political, and technological implications from the emergence and growth of the financial services industry.

This permeation of finance into the economic, social, and political life of a city, country or even region is broadly known as 'financialisation',[3] or the "increasing role of financial motives, financial markets, financial actors and financial institutions in the operation of domestic and international economies".[4] More than simply a shift from 'real' economic activities such as manufacturing and trade to financial activities, financialisation involves the permeation of finance into every aspect of economic, social, and political life, and often the *replacement* of real economic activities with financial ones.[5]

In many cases, Singapore included, financialisation is often driven by a combination of financial innovation and deregulation, which, for better or worse, encourages the creation and sustenance of new financial instruments.[6] As a city-state, Singapore retains both the trappings of a city and a country, multiple layers of political and policy processes compressed within its small geographical size. This has greatly facilitated the financialisation of its economic, sociopolitical spheres. These will be discussed in the rest of this chapter.

Financialisation and the Economy

As the world's third most competitive financial centre,[7] there is little doubt that the financial services sector plays a crucial role in Singapore's economy. As mentioned above, the financial services sector accounts for 12.6% of Singapore's GDP. More importantly, it continues to hold strong growth prospects. For the year 2015, Singapore's finance and insurance industry contributed to one-third — or 0.7 percentage points — of Singapore's 2% GDP growth that year.[8]

In short, financial services make up a major proportion of economic activities in Singapore, and they are expected to continue doing so for the foreseeable future. This is evident in the large numbers of financial institutions operating in the city-state. As of December 2016, there are 126 commercial banks operating in Singapore (with 121 of them being foreign banks), 266 registered fund management companies, 183 licensed insurers, and 569 licensed providers of capital market services.[9]

In particular, Singapore has registered strong growth in its asset management and insurance industries. As of the end 2015, assets under management in Singapore stand at S$2.6 trillion — a near ten-fold increase from the S$276.2 billion of assets that were under management in the year 2000.[10] The insurance industry similarly registered strong growth over the same period, with total industry assets growing from S$45,409.8 million in 2000 to S$202,748.6 million in 2015.[11] On a year-on-year basis, assets under management grew by 9% in 2015,[12] while the general insurance industry experienced a 2.6% growth in total gross premiums in the same year.[13]

There has, in short, been substantial growth and expansion of Singapore's financial services sector, with the number of financial institutions operating in Singapore and the levels of assets handled by these institutions continuing to register strong growth. Furthermore, the financial services sector has expanded not only in size, but complexity and sophistication as well, with specific niches emerging to become key value propositions for Singapore. These niches include asset management, foreign currency exchange (forex), commodities, and banking.[14]

Indeed, the asset management and insurance industries continue to be perceived as a potential area of growth for Singapore, with the city-state's sociopolitical stability and regulatory transparency proving attractive to high net worth individuals (HNWIs) and investors from all over the world,[15] and structural conditions such as the continued rise of regional wealth and Asia's relatively low insurance penetration rate (when compared to advanced economies) promising to drive further growth in the asset management and insurance industries.[16]

The strength of Singapore's financial services sector stands in stark contrast to its manufacturing sector, which saw a decline of 3.6% in manufacturing output in 2016.[17] Indeed, the manufacturing sector's share of Singapore's GDP has steadily declined from 27.7% in 2000 to 18.4% in 2014.[18] There has, in other words, been a steady decline in Singapore's manufacturing sector, even as the financial services sector continues to experience strong growth. This growth of the financial services sector at the expense of manufacturing is not simply limited to market size and growth levels.

Given the limited size of Singapore's population, and hence labour force, there has been increasing competition for skilled talent. In particular, a sizeable proportion of university graduates are gravitating towards the financial services sector due to the more attractive remuneration packages offered.[19] As Table 3.1 shows, the employment distribution of the services sector (as a percentage of total employment) has risen steadily, while that of manufacturing has experienced a steep decline. The finance and insurance services sector currently make up 5.5% of Singapore's total employment.[20]

Hence, and as is the case in many of countries, financialisation has come at the expense of real economic activities such as manufacturing, with investments and human

Table 3.1: Employment Distributions of Manufacturing and Services Sectors

Employment Distribution (% of Total Employment)	2006	2007	2008	2009	2010	2011	2012	2013	2014	2015
Manufacturing	20.7	20.8	19.9	17.4	16.7	16.2	15.9	15.5	14.8	14.1
Services	68.4	67.7	67.3	69.2	70.3	70.6	70.2	70.1	70.9	71.5

Adapted from Ministry of Manpower (2016), Summary Table: Employment[21]

capital diverted from the real economy to the financial services sector. This has significant implications for Singapore's approach towards economic development. In particular, there has been a shift in focus from the export of goods to the search for 'exportable services',[22] the likes of which can be found in the financial services sector or the more recent technological start-up industry.

As such, financialisation does not obviate Singapore's perennial need to ensure economic development and stimulate growth. Rather, and in providing the possibility of finance as a form of 'exportable service', it remains embedded within Singapore's developmental focus. Hence, despite the relative decline of manufacturing, there remains a strong focus on Singapore's 'export-led' approach to generating economic growth, although the focus has shifted from exporting manufactured goods to delivering exportable services.

In fact, this shift is often perceived to be a deliberate one, with its roots attributed to Singapore's post-independence desire in 1967 to develop the financial services sector as a second 'engine' of growth, especially in light of its lack of a natural economic hinterland.[23] However, it was only well into the 1980s that Singapore's financial services sector took on its international character and the 2000s that it truly began to show signs of rivalling other real economic activities as a major driver of economic growth and source of employment.[24]

There has, in short, been a rapid financialisation of Singapore's economy, with the financial services sector expanding rapidly and threatening to eventually eclipse the city-state's traditional manufacturing sector, whether in terms of industry size, contribution to GDP, or share of employment. Furthermore, the rapid growth of consumer finance has resulted in the permeation of banks and financial institutions into the everyday landscape of Singapore's heartlands, with citizens gaining access to increasingly sophisticated investments and financial instruments, albeit with a corresponding heightened exposure to risk.[25]

However, the financialisation that Singapore has experienced over the past few decades is qualitatively different from that in other countries. While financialisation has often imbued financial institutions and international organisations with power and authority over a country's policy and political processes,[26] this has not happened in Singapore. Rather, the state remains very much in control of financialisation, although financial institutions have also gained some level of entry into the government's policy processes. The impacts of financialisation of Singapore's sociopolitical context are discussed next.

Sociopolitical Implications

With the growing influence of financial firms and the emergence of social categories such as the 'financial subject' or 'financial citizen', finance has permeated into many aspects of political decision-making and citizenship in many countries all over the world. Indeed, it is often noted that financial institutions exert a disproportionate level of influence over political leaders and policymakers, through what is known as 'regulatory capture'.[27] By 'capturing' regulators and policymakers, financial institutions are able to influence policy outcomes towards their advantage, and extract economic benefits from these outcomes.

However, such regulatory capture can cause instability in the financial system, and even result in crises.[28] Aside from regulatory capture, finance is also strongly related to politics in terms of the *a priori* sociopolitical configurations and political systemic conditions that exist before the emergence of the financial services sector in any given city, and which continue to impact the ways in which the city's economic structure and financial services sector are structured and developed.[29]

These conditions determine structural factors such as the presence of politically connected market incumbents, the hospitability of prevailing economic conditions for new market entrants, and the availability of resources to both incumbents and new entrants, among others. This linkage between initial sociopolitical conditions and subsequent financial sector development is also dynamic and reiterative, often resulting in new configurations of financial sector stakeholders and their relations with policymakers, as these initial conditions are modified or give rise to new sociopolitical interactions and dynamics.

In the case of Singapore, such *a priori* political conditions have proven fortuitous. As a former British colonial outpost, Singapore retained its British-styled common law system, constitution, and public administration even after independence. Indeed, these elements have largely remained intact, receiving only slight modifications to accommodate shifting policy conditions.[30] Specifically, Singapore's common law system and political stability have been seen as key advantages that continue to drive its success as a global financial centre.[31]

Political stability and legal transparency are factors that tend to be highly valued by investors and financial institutions that are seeking safe haven for their investments. Singapore's political stability and commitment to rule of law are particularly pertinent, especially in light of the geopolitical instability that has mired the Southeast and East Asian regions in the past few decades.

Aside from structural conditions, financialisation also gives rise to sociopolitical implications at the individual level. Specifically, the permeation of financial institutions into the everyday lives and living environs of ordinary citizens has resulted in what is known as 'financial subjectivisation', whereby the identities and activities of individuals are increasingly influenced by and ultimately subsumed within the financial activities that they participate in, whether these be personal finance or insurance.[32]

In sum, there are significant sociopolitical implications of financialisation for cities, their political leaders and policymakers, and citizens. Given the rapid emergence and expansion of its financial services sector, how do these sociopolitical implications impact Singapore, if at all?

At the policy level, Singapore has proven itself to be remarkably resistant to regulatory capture and other efforts to influence or subvert its financial policy processes. This is evident in the strong standing of its financial regulatory and governance processes on global rankings of economies and financial centres.[33] Indeed, Singapore has been ranked highly for the transparency of its political infrastructure and policy processes in the Global Competitiveness Report 2015–2016.[34]

Aside from the transparency of its overall political and policy processes, Singapore's resistance to regulatory capture is more fundamentally driven by the efforts of its chief financial regulator, the Monetary Authority of Singapore (MAS). Through its flexible 'risk-focused' approach, the MAS ensures the stability of Singapore's financial markets and the soundness of its institutions, and at the same time, provides the necessary space for financial innovation and competitiveness.[35] This combination of high regulatory standards with flexible implementation has been described as "smart regulation".[36]

From an organisational perspective, the MAS reports directly to the Prime Minister's Office (PMO). While this means that the MAS is not strictly an 'independent' regulator, in the way that mainstream economics understands it, housing the MAS under the supervision of the PMO helps ensure that financial regulatory activities are geared towards national interests, rather than private ones. Furthermore, the MAS was established as a 'statutory board'. Statutory boards are semi-autonomous agencies that assist the civil service in the provision or implementation of certain public services.

Despite their 'semi-autonomous' status, most statutory boards in Singapore remain embedded within the overall governing milieu of the Singapore government, and hence, operate as policy arms of the government.[37] Given Singapore's continued adherence to the developmental state model, this also means that statutory boards, like most of Singapore's public agencies, are relatively insulated from social pressures and private lobbying efforts.[38] In short, financial regulation in Singapore is highly centralised, state-driven, and relatively insulated from industry influence.

However, this is not to suggest a complete lack of interactions between the MAS and private sector financial institutions. Rather, there is a significant amount of industry consultation in the MAS's policymaking processes, with financial institutions and other industry actors frequently consulted on both the form and content of the MAS's financial regulations and policies.[39] Much of this consultation takes place through the formation of formal advisory and consultative committees, such as the Economic Review Committee, which was first introduced in the 1980s, or the more recent Future Economy Dialogues.[40]

These formal consultative committees provide the MAS with a closer understanding of industry concerns, expectations, and projections for the future. However, these formal avenues of state-industry interactions only tell half the story. The MAS also consults industry actors on an informal and continuous basis, forming strong and dynamic relationships with these industry actors.[41] The result of this is the formation of dense 'policy relations' between the MAS and private sector financial institutions.[42] As such, the financialisation of Singapore's economy and the emergence of its vibrant financial service sector has been accompanied by the formation of close sociopolitical relations between its financial regulators and industry actors.

These relations are especially important when seen in light of the MAS's role as developmental agency for Singapore's financial services sector. Aside from its traditional roles as central bank and chief financial regulator, the MAS is also, by virtue of its strong financial sector domain knowledge, the apex developmental agency for Singapore's financial services sector.[43] This developmental role involves identifying potential growth areas or 'niches' in Singapore's financial sector and introducing various 'sweeteners' such as subsidies in order to develop these areas.[44]

At the individual level, scholars and analysts have noted the permeation of finance into the heartlands, with individual and household decisions often influenced or driven by financial interests and concerns, especially in terms of insurance, personal finance, and other investment instruments. This has resulted in what is often described as the financial 'subjectivisation', or the creation of 'financial subjects', as the everyday lives of citizens become increasingly within the operating logics of investment and finance.[45]

Much of this began with the introduction of the Central Provident Fund Investment Scheme in 1986, which allowed citizens to invest a portion of their retirement funds in selected funds and equities.[46] This was further compounded by the provision of sophisticated financial services by mass-market 'neighbourhood' banks such as the Post Office Savings Bank (POSB), which was a former public savings bank and still continues to play its key role as a mass-market savings bank.[47]

However, financial subjectivisation can also come with risks and other adverse implications for citizens. For instance, the purchase of Lehman 'minibonds' by retired or middle-aged individuals with their life savings resulted in their exposure to the global financial crisis.[48] As is the case in high finance, risk and investments have become ubiquitous elements of a citizen's financial decisions, as the focus has gradually shifted from 'saving for a rainy day' to making good returns on one's assets, whether these be cash savings or property.

Furthermore, the pace of financial subjectivisation has been quickened by the emergence of financial technologies that provide citizens with even greater access to financial instruments and investments. Aside from citizens, such financial technologies, or 'FinTech', have also generated profound shifts and transformations Singapore's financial services sector and brought forth significant opportunities for banks and financial institutions. This emerging confluence of technology and financialisation is discussed in the following section.

FinTech: Technologising Financialisation?

Aside from the economic and sociopolitical factors discussed above, there are also strong technological implications arising from financialisation. In particular, the confluence of Singapore's highly developed financial sector with its burgeoning technology start-up sector has given rise to the emergence of FinTech start-ups in Singapore. Indeed, Singapore has been ranked fourth among the world's FinTech hubs by the consultancy EY.[49] It is generally perceived to be pulling ahead of close rival Hong Kong to emerge as Asia's leading FinTech hub.[50]

Before discussing Singapore's financialisation-driven rise as a leading FinTech hub, there is first a need to establish a working understanding of FinTech. As a concept, FinTech is notoriously broad.

While FinTech initially referred to the application of technology to back-end operations of consumer and trade financial institutions, the increasing sophistication and rapid expansion of the internet as well as mobile internet applications has expanded the ambit of FinTech considerably to include "any technological innovation in the financial sector, including innovations in financial literacy and education, retail banking, investment and even crypto-currencies like Bitcoin".[51] Indeed, it is by no means an exaggeration to say that there are as many forms of FinTech as there are different ways of applying technology to finance.

Several technological innovations have proven especially relevant to FinTech applications. These include data analytics, algorithm-based tools such as 'robo-advisors' and automated banking, and open database platforms such as distributed ledgers or blockchain. While robo-advisors and automated banking were developed to enhance customer experience, tools such as data analytics and blockchain are geared towards reducing information asymmetry and transaction costs for financial institutions as well as other users of financial services.

More importantly, the emergence of FinTech has been associated with potential disruption to the traditional banking and finance industry. A recently published Citigroup report notes that FinTech is changing the relationships that banks have with their customers, with customers increasingly relying on digital options such as internet banking, rather than walking into a physical bank branch, for their banking needs.[52] This has significant implications for the prospects and profitability of traditional financial institutions.

According to the same report, approximately 17% of US consumer bank revenue — or US$1,200 billion — is expected to migrate to digitally enabled business models such as FinTech start-ups.[53] Furthermore, the disruptive potential of FinTech is not evenly spread across different financial services and institutions. For instance, personal loans, digital payments, wealth management, and small and medium-sized business loans are expected to face greater disruption than other financial services.[54]

While the emergence and expansion of FinTech would not have been possible without the technological innovations that have made the various FinTech business models and transactions possible, financialisation remains the key underlying driving force of FinTech. Indeed, a big part of the allure of adopting FinTech innovations arguably derives from the ability of these innovations or technologies to make financial transactions more efficient as well as the business opportunities that these innovations present to both emerging start-ups and existing financial institutions.

In short, FinTech remains very much entrenched within the financial and economic logics of financialisation. While earlier phases of financialisation had involved the intrusion of finance into the everyday life of citizens through the introduction of personal and consumer banking as well as the physical location of bank branches and ATMs within the living environs of citizens, the emergence of FinTech portends a second and even more intensive wave of financialisation.

This is particularly the case, with the growing ubiquity of internet and mobile technologies that allow citizens to access their bank accounts or enact a financial transaction from wherever they happen to be. Indeed, the introduction of internet and mobile banking has allowed financialisation to permeate ever deeper into the personal space of individuals. While earlier phases of financialisation had involved the gradual invasion of finance into neighbourhoods, FinTech has allowed financialisation to move into the homes and workplaces of citizens.

These forces and elements are particularly pronounced in Singapore, which boasts of high mobile and internet penetration rates. Singapore's mobile penetration rate rose from 95.8% in June 2006 to 149.1% in April 2016,[55] while the total number of broadband subscriptions increased from 684,600 in June 2006 to 12.1689 million in April 2016.[56] In light of the growing digitisation of Singapore's population, the government unveiled its 'Smart Nation' initiative in 2014, which aims to address urban policy issues through the use of data and technological solutions.[57]

An important component of Singapore's ambition to become a smart nation is its 'smart financial centre' drive, which emphasises the application of digital and data technologies among both financial institutions and regulators.[58] Hence, taken within the context of the Smart Nation initiative and the smart financial centre drive, the emergence and growth of FinTech in Singapore has thus far been largely state-driven.

In particular, the government has devoted significant levels of resources to develop Singapore's burgeoning FinTech industry. Similar to past efforts at developing potential financial sector growth areas, this has often involved the provision of tax benefits, government support, and market access to FinTech firms.[59] However, there is also a qualitative difference in the government's approach towards developing the FinTech industry, as compared to other past efforts. In particular, there has been a greater emphasis on systemic variables, such as the need for a vibrant start-up ecosystem.

For instance, a FinTech regulatory sandbox was developed and introduced by the MAS to provide start-ups with a safe environment within which they can test out their ideas and products, without posing unnecessary risk to Singapore's financial system. This was complemented by the establishment of Looking Glass @ MAS, a FinTech innovation lab located within the MAS that allows the MAS to experiment FinTech solutions with financial institutions and start-ups.[60] More recently, the MAS unveiled a new scheme that will fund up to half the cost of promising FinTech "proof-of-concept" trials, with the maximum for each project set at S$200,000.[61]

There has, as such, been strong efforts by the Singapore government to foster and encourage the development of its FinTech industry. Furthermore, such efforts are predicated upon the assumption that FinTech will sustain, and even drive, the continued success of Singapore's financial services sector by providing new business opportunities for financial institutions and enhancing customer experiences of financial services.[62] Seen in this light, FinTech represents a *continuation* of financialisation in Singapore, rather than the emergence of a new industry qualitatively different from traditional banking and finance.

Conclusion

This chapter has discussed the various aspects of financialisation in Singapore. Indeed, being the second element of this book's conceptualisation of the global financial centre, financialisation is crucial in defining the specific activities that take place within any given financial city. As discussed above, financialisation often involves the supplanting of real economic activities, such as manufacturing and exports, with financial activities. In many cases, this coincides with a city's shift from being a port-city to becoming a financial centre.

This was certainly the case in Singapore, with the financial services sector growing in size and as share of Singapore's GDP. It is also becoming a major source of employment. While trade and manufacturing continue to play important roles in Singapore's economy, the reality is that the manufacturing sector has been steadily declining over the years, while the financial services sector has been growing rapidly. There is therefore a very real possibility of finance overtaking manufacturing as Singapore's major growth industry.

There are also physical and existential dimensions to financialisation. For instance, the rapid expansion of the financial hub within most global cities has resulted in the appropriation of prime real estate within the city centre for financial purposes, often extending into waterfront areas that have previously been the sites of trade and manufacturing activities. This is evident even in Singapore's waterfront, with former warehouses along Clark Quay now housing dining and entertainment establishments that cater to the financial sector professionals who work just a stone's throw away.

More fundamentally, financialisation tends to affect the sociocultural complexion of a city, especially through operations of financial subjectivisation. Hence, as a city transforms itself into a global financial centre, so too do its inhabitants experience the allure of finance as both a career option and a means of enhancing personal savings and assets. The growing political clout of financial institutions serves to round out this *mea culpa*, with domestic politics increasingly centred on financial sector interests.

In the case of Singapore, such political forces are blunted by the institutional strength of the MAS and the transparency of its regulations. However, financial subjectivisation is indeed occurring at a rapid pace, with citizens increasingly financialising their savings and assets, and financial institutions developing more products targeted at consumer and retail banking. As this chapter has discussed, the logic (and risks) of finance has slowly permeated into the everyday lives and psyche of ordinary citizens.

Finally, the emergence of advanced digital technological innovations has facilitated the rapid growth of Singapore's FinTech industry. However, and as I have discussed above, technology is not the only enabling factor for Singapore's FinTech industry. Rather, the emergence and growth of FinTech in Singapore remains driven by the logic of financialisation, albeit aided by active government support and intervention. Indeed, the adoption of FinTech solutions and technologies is predicated upon a desire among both financial institutions and consumers of financial services to derive the economic gains of getting greater access to a more diverse range of financial services.

Seen in this light, FinTech represents a continuation of an ongoing process of financialisation in Singapore's broader political economy, with the apparatuses, logics, and structures that have traditionally facilitated financialisation now enhanced and mediated by new digital and data technologies. Yet, even as we note the central role of financialisation in Singapore's development as a global financial centre, there is also a need to emphasise the spatial centralisation of financial activities within the confines of the city. This is discussed in the next chapter.

Endnotes

1. Department of Statistics Singapore, "Share of GDP by Industry," February 25, 2016, http://www.singstat.gov.sg/statistics/visualising-data/charts/share-of-gdp-by-industry.
2. Natasha Hamilton-Hart, *Asian States, Asian Bankers: Central Banking in Southeast Asia* (New York: Cornell University Press, 2002); J. J. Woo, *Singapore as an International Financial Centre: History, Politics and Policy* (London: Palgrave Macmillan, 2016); J. J. Woo, *Business and Politics in Asia's Key Financial Centres — Hong Kong, Singapore and Shanghai*, 1st ed. (Singapore: Springer, 2016).
3. Greta R. Krippner, "The Financialization of the American Economy," *Socio-Economic Review* 3, No. 2 (May 1, 2005): 173–208; Sarah Hall, "Geographies of Money and Finance II: Financialization and Financial Subjects," *Progress in Human Geography* 36, No. 3 (2012): 403–411; Mark Kear, "Governing Homo Subprimicus: Beyond Financial Citizenship, Exclusion, and Rights," *Antipode* 45, No. 4 (September 1, 2013): 926–946; Karen P. Y. Lai and Choon Hang Tan, "'Neighbours First, Bankers Second': Mobilising Financial Citizenship in Singapore," *Geoforum* 64 (August 2015): 65–77.

4. Gerald A. Epstein, *Financialization and the World Economy* (Cheltenham, UK: Edward Elgar Publishing, 2005), p. 3.
5. Krippner, "The Financialization of the American Economy"; Hall, "Geographies of Money and Finance II"; Kear, "Governing Homo Subprimicus"; Lai and Tan, "'Neighbours First, Bankers Second.'"
6. Domna M. Michailidou, *The Inexorable Evolution of Financialisation: Financial Crises in Emerging Markets* (London: Palgrave Macmillan, 2016), p. 49.
7. Mark Yeandle, "Global Financial Centre Index 19" (London, U.K.: Z/Yen Group and Qatar Financial Centre Authority, March 2016).
8. The Straits Times, "Singapore's Financial Services Sector Resilient amid New Challenges," *The Straits Times*, March 16, 2016.
9. Monetary Authority of Singapore, "Financial Directory," *MASNET*, December 7, 2016, https://masnetsvc.mas.gov.sg/FID.html.
10. Monetary Authority of Singapore, "2000 Survey of the Singapore Asset Management Industry" (Singapore: Monetary Authority of Singapore, 2000); Monetary Authority of Singapore, "2015 Singapore Asset Management Survey: Singapore — Global City, World of Opportunities" (Singapore: Monetary Authority of Singapore, 2015).
11. Monetary Authority of Singapore, "Insurance Statistics 2015," November 26, 2016, http://www.mas.gov.sg/Statistics/Insurance-Statistics/Annual-Statistics/Insurance-Statistics-2015.aspx.
12. Monetary Authority of Singapore, "2015 Singapore Asset Management Survey: Singapore — Global City, World of Opportunities."
13. Channel NewsAsia, "Singapore's General Insurance Industry Saw Premiums Rise to S$3.6b in 2015," *Channel NewsAsia*, March 17, 2016, http://www.channelnewsasia.com/news/business/singapore/singapore-s-general/2610590.html.
14. J. J. Woo, *Business and Politics in Asia's Key Financial Centres — Hong Kong, Singapore and Shanghai.*
15. Yvonne Guo and Jun Jie Woo, "Wealth Management for All Seasons," *The Straits Times*, December 3, 2013, http://www.academia.edu/6087604/Wealth_Management_for_All_Seasons; Yvonne Guo and J. J. Woo, *Singapore and Switzerland: Secrets to Small State Success* (New Jersey: World Scientific Publishing Co., 2016).
16. *The Straits Times*, "Singapore's Financial Services Sector Resilient amid New Challenges."
17. See Kit Tang, "Singapore's Manufacturing Output Falls 3.6% in July, First Contraction in 5 Months," *Channel NewsAsia*, August 26, 2016, http://www.channelnewsasia.com/news/business/singapore/singapore-s-manufacturing/3075904.html.
18. Department of Statistics Singapore, "Share of GDP by Industry."
19. Janice Heng, "Fresh Graduates Banking on Finance Sector for Jobs," *The Straits Times*, July 8, 2013, http://www.straitstimes.com/singapore/fresh-graduates-banking-on-finance-sector-for-jobs.

20. Ministry of Manpower, "Distribution of Employment by Industry," *Ministry of Manpower Singapore*, September 21, 2016, http://stats.mom.gov.sg/Pages/Employment-Distribution-and-Employment-Level-by-Industry.aspx.
21. Ministry of Manpower, "Summary Table: Employment," *Ministry of Manpower Singapore*, September 14, 2016, http://stats.mom.gov.sg/Pages/Employment-Summary-Table.aspx.
22. J. J. Woo, *Business and Politics in Asia's Key Financial Centres — Hong Kong, Singapore and Shanghai*, p. 86.
23. Manuel F. Montes, "Tokyo, Hong Kong and Singapore as Competing Financial Centres," *Journal of Asian Business* 18, No. 1 (1999): 153–168; Kuan Yew Lee, *From Third World to First: The Singapore Story: 1965–2000* (Singapore: Times Editions, 2000); Ian Patrick Austin, *Goh Keng Swee And Southeast Asian Governance* (Singapore: Marshall Cavendish Academic, 2004); Linda Low, *The Political Economy of a City-State Revised* (Singapore: Marshall Cavendish, 2006); J. J. Woo, *Singapore as an International Financial Centre: History, Politics and Policy*.
24. J. J. Woo, *Business and Politics in Asia's Key Financial Centres — Hong Kong, Singapore and Shanghai*; J. J. Woo, *Singapore as an International Financial Centre: History, Politics and Policy*.
25. Karen P. Y. Lai, "The Lehman Minibonds Crisis and Financialisation of Investor Subjects in Singapore," *Area* 45, No. 3 (September 1, 2013): 273–282, doi:10.1111/area.12040; Lai and Tan, "'Neighbours First, Bankers Second.'"
26. Toby Carroll and Darryl S. L. Jarvis, "Introduction: Financialisation and Development in Asia under Late Capitalism," *Asian Studies Review* 38, No. 4 (October 2, 2014): 533–543; Andrew Baker, "Restraining Regulatory Capture? Anglo-America, Crisis Politics and Trajectories of Change in Global Financial Governance," *International Affairs* 86, No. 3 (2010): 647–663.
27. Michael E. Levine and Jennifer L. Forrence, "Regulatory Capture, Public Interest, and the Public Agenda: Toward a Synthesis," *Journal of Law, Economics, & Organization* 6 (1990): 167–198; Jean-Jacques Laffont and Jean Tirole, "The Politics of Government Decision-Making: A Theory of Regulatory Capture," *The Quarterly Journal of Economics* 106, No. 4 (1991): 1089–1127, doi:10.2307/2937958; Ernesto Dal Bó, "Regulatory Capture: A Review," *Oxford Review of Economic Policy* 22, No. 2 (June 20, 2006): 203–225; Baker, "Restraining Regulatory Capture?"
28. Baker, "Restraining Regulatory Capture?"; Stijn Claessens and Laura Kodres, "The Regulatory Responses to the Global Financial Crisis: Some Uncomfortable Questions," IMF Working Paper (Washington, D.C.: International Monetary Fund, March 2014); Stijn Claessens *et al.*, *Financial Crises: Causes, Consequences, and Policy Responses* (International Monetary Fund, 2014).
29. Stephen Haggard and Chung H. Lee, "The Political Dimension of Finance in Economic Development," in *The Politics of Finance in Developing Countries*, ed. Stephen Haggard, Chung H. Lee, and Sylvia Maxfield (New York: Cornell University Press, 1993), pp. 3–20; Stephen Haggard, Chung H. Lee, and Sylvia Maxfield, *The Politics of Finance in Developing Countries* (Cornell University Press, 1993); Richard

W. Carney, "The Political Economy of Financial Systems," SSRN Scholarly Paper (Rochester, NY: Social Science Research Network, November 1, 2001), http://papers.ssrn.com/abstract=2165154; Richard W Carney, *Contested Capitalism: The Political Origins of Financial Institutions* (London: Routledge, 2010).

30. Jon S. T. Quah, *Public Administration Singapore-Style* (Singapore: Emerald Group Publishing, 2010).
31. J. J. Woo, *Business and Politics in Asia's Key Financial Centres — Hong Kong, Singapore and Shanghai*, p. 124.
32. Hall, "Geographies of Money and Finance II"; Karen P. Y. Lai, "Financial Advisors, Financial Ecologies and the Variegated Financialisation of Everyday Investors," *Transactions of the Institute of British Geographers* 41, No. 1 (January 1, 2016): 27–40, doi:10.1111/tran.12101; Niamh Mulcahy, "Entrepreneurial Subjectivity and the Political Economy of Daily Life in the Time of Finance," *European Journal of Social Theory*, June 21, 2016, 1368431016655074, doi:10.1177/1368431016655074.
33. Dennis Brandes *et al.*, "Deloitte Global Wealth Management Centre Ranking 2015" (Zurich, Switzerland: Deloitte Consulting AG, 2015); IMD, "World Competitiveness Yearbook 2016" (Lausanne: IMD, 2016); Klaus Schwab, "The Global Competitiveness Report 2015–2016" (Geneva: World Economic Forum, 2016); Yeandle, "Global Financial Centre Index 19."
34. Schwab, "The Global Competitiveness Report 2015–2016"; Economic Development Board, "Facts and Rankings," *Singapore Economic Development Board — Investing Business in Singapore*, October 7, 2016, https://www.edb.gov.sg/content/edb/en/why-singapore/about-singapore/facts-and-rankings/rankings.html.
35. Hsien Loong Lee, "New Approach to Regulating and Developing Singapore's Financial Sector" (Speech by DPM Lee Hsien Loong, SESDAQ 10th Anniversary Dinner, Singapore, November 4, 1997); Der Jiun Chia, "Objectives and Principles of Financial Supervision in Singapore," in *Regulation and the Limits of Competition*, Economics Symposium Series 1 (Singapore: SNP International Publishing Pte. Ltd., 2007), pp. 44–58.
36. Ravi Menon, "Singapore's Financial Centre in the New Landscape" (Investment Management Association of Singapore (IMAS) 14th Annual Conference, Singapore, March 13, 2013), http://www.mas.gov.sg/News-and-Publications/Monetary-Policy-Statements-and-Speeches/2013/Singapore-Financial-Centre-in-the-New-Landscape.aspx.
37. J. J. Woo, "Singapore's Policy Style: Statutory Boards as Policymaking Units," *Journal of Asian Public Policy* 8, No. 2 (2014): 120–133.
38. W.G. Huff, "The Developmental State, Government, and Singapore's Economic Development since 1960," *World Development* 23, No. 8 (August 1995): 1421–1438; Martin Perry, *Singapore: A Developmental City State* (Chichester: Wiley, 1997); Linda Low, "The Singapore Developmental State in the New Economy and Polity," *The Pacific Review* 14, No. 3 (January 1, 2001): 411–441.
39. J. J. Woo, "Beyond the Neoliberal Orthodoxy: Alternative Financial Policy Regimes in Asia's Financial Centres," *Critical Policy Studies* 9, No. 3 (2015): 297–316; J. J. Woo, *Business and Politics in Asia's Key Financial Centres — Hong Kong, Singapore*

and Shanghai; J. J. Woo, *Singapore as an International Financial Centre: History, Politics and Policy*.

40. Economic Review Committee, "Positioning Singapore as a Pre-Eminent Financial Centre in Asia," *Financial Services Working Group Report* (Singapore: Ministry of Trade and Industry, 2003); National Library Board Singapore, "Establishment of the Economic Review Committee — Singapore History," *History SG*, 2016, http://eresources.nlb.gov.sg/history/events/459b32e3-35c3-4112-9042-94aaa9c13057; Committee on the Future of Economy Secretariat, "Committee On The Future Economy To Review Singapore's Economic Strategies and Position Us For The Future," Press Release (Singapore: Ministry of Finance, December 21, 2015), http://www.mof.gov.sg/news-reader/articleid/1565/parentId/59/year/2015?category=Press%20Releases.
41. Ravi Menon, Interview, September 26, 2013.
42. J. J. Woo, "Policy Relations and Policy Subsystems: Financial Policy in Hong Kong and Singapore," *International Journal of Public Administration* 38, No. 8 (2015): 553–561.
43. Yong Guan Koh, Interview, August 7, 2013.
44. Ravi Menon, Interview; J. J. Woo, *Business and Politics in Asia's Key Financial Centres — Hong Kong, Singapore and Shanghai*; J. J. Woo, *Singapore as an International Financial Centre: History, Politics and Policy*.
45. Hall, "Geographies of Money and Finance II"; Lai, "The Lehman Minibonds Crisis and Financialisation of Investor Subjects in Singapore"; Ray Forrest and Yosuke Hirayama, "The Financialisation of the Social Project: Embedded Liberalism, Neoliberalism and Home Ownership," *Urban Studies*, April 3, 2014, http://usj.sagepub.com/content/early/2014/04/02/0042098014528394; Lai, "Financial Advisors, Financial Ecologies and the Variegated Financialisation of Everyday Investors."
46. Lai, "The Lehman Minibonds Crisis and Financialisation of Investor Subjects in Singapore," pp. 274–275; Central Provident Fund Board, "CPFIS," *CPF Website*, September 7, 2016, https://www.cpf.gov.sg/members/bptopics/bp-topics/cpfis.
47. Lai and Tan, '*Neighbours First, Bankers Second*.'
48. Lai, *The Lehman Minibonds Crisis and Financialisation of Investor Subjects in Singapore*.
49. EY, "UK FinTech On the Cutting Edge an Evaluation of the International FinTech Sector" (London, U.K.: EY, 2016).
50. Chanyaporn Chanjaroen and Darren Boey, "Singapore Is Beating Hong Kong in Asia's Fintech Race," *Bloomberg*, December 7, 2016, https://www.bloomberg.com/news/articles/2016-12-07/with-fintech-rising-hong-kong-singapore-rivalry-gets-new-twist.
51. Investopedia, "Fintech," *Investopedia*, March 17, 2015, http://www.investopedia.com/terms/f/fintech.asp.
52. Citi, "Digital Disruption: How FinTech Is Forcing Banks to a Tipping Point," Citi GPS: Global Perspectives & Solutions (New York, N.Y.: Citigroup, March 2016), p. 3.

53. *Ibid*, p. 21.
54. *Ibid*, p. 22.
55. Government of Singapore, "Mobile Penetration Rate," *Data.gov.sg*, December 14, 2016, https://data.gov.sg/dataset/mobile-penetration-rate.
56. Government of Singapore, "Number of Broadband Subscriptions by Type, Annual," *Data.gov.sg*, December 14, 2016, https://data.gov.sg/dataset/number-of-broadband-subscriptions-by-type-annual?resource_id=949a1766-8b8a-438f-8d61-c70173cb6c58.
57. Hsien Loong Lee, "Smart Nation: Better Living, More Opportunities, Stronger Communities" (Prime Minister Lee Hsien Loong's speech at Smart Nation launch, Singapore, November 24, 2014); Infocomm Development Authority of Singapore, "Singapore Lays Groundwork to Be World's First Smart Nation," News Release (Singapore: Infocomm Development Authority of Singapore, June 18, 2014), http://www.ida.gov.sg/blog/insg/featured/singapore-lays-groundwork-to-be-worlds-first-smart-nation/; Smart Nation Programme Office, "About Smart Nation," 2016, http://www.smartnation.sg/about-smart-nation.
58. Ravi Menon, "A Smart Financial Centre" (Keynote Address, Global Technology Law Conference 2015, Singapore, June 29, 2015), http://www.mas.gov.sg/news-and-publications/speeches-and-monetary-policy-statements/speeches/2015/a-smart-financial-centre.aspx.
59. Chanjaroen and Boey, *Singapore Is Beating Hong Kong in Asia's Fintech Race.*
60. Monetary Authority of Singapore, "MAS Establishes FinTech Innovation Lab," Press Release (Singapore: Monetary Authority of Singapore, August 24, 2016), http://www.mas.gov.sg/News-and-Publications/Media-Releases/2016/MAS-establishes-FinTech-Innovation-Lab.aspx.
61. Yasmine Yahya, "Singapore's push to be fintech hub," *The Straits Times*, November 22, 2016, http://www.straitstimes.com/business/companies-markets/singapores-push-to-be-fintech-hub.
62. Tharman Shanmugaratnam, "Speech at the Launch of the Singapore FinTech Festival" (Speech, Launch of the Singapore FinTech Festival at the Asia Society, New York, N.Y., April 12, 2016), http://www.mas.gov.sg/News-and-Publications/Speeches-and-Monetary-Policy-Statements/Speeches/2016/Speech-at-the-Launch-of-the-Singapore-FinTech-Festival.aspx.

THERE WAS NO NATURAL REASON WHY A BROAD RANGE OF GLOBAL FINANCIAL INSTITUTIONS AND SERVICES HAD TO BE LOCATED IN SINGAPORE, A SMALL ISLAND STATE SEPARATED FROM ITS MALAYAN HINTERLAND.

THARMAN SHANMUGARATNAM
KEYNOTE ADDRESS AT THE ASSOCIATION OF BANKS IN SINGAPORE (ABS) ANNUAL DINNER
30 JUNE 2015

CHAPTER FOUR

Making Sure the Centre Holds

The past two chapters have discussed the two processes of globalisation and financialisation, and how these two processes have driven Singapore's development as a global financial centre. However, these two processes do not, on their own, sufficiently explain *why* or *how* it is that financial institutions and activities have come to converge upon the 719.1 square kilometres of landmass that is Singapore, and chosen to remain there. In fact, globalisation and financialisation would paradoxically predict the opposite — the spatial diffusion, rather than centralisation, of economic and financial activities over space.

Indeed, the advent of globalisation, when combined with the proliferation of advanced ICT technologies, has heralded the beginning of what some have termed the "borderless" economy.[1] What this means is that business transactions and economic activities can now, through the internet and other communications technologies such as teleconferencing, take place across national boundaries without the need for face-to-face interactions among its participants. It is therefore now possible to disaggregate supply chains and other business operations across multiple jurisdictions.[2]

Financialisation, which has led to a growing emphasis on financial activities over real economic activities, has served to further perpetuate this alleged negation of physical space and territoriality. Increasingly, economic activity and transactions are taking place over stock exchanges, and physical assets becoming converted into tradable and highly fungible financial assets and instruments. The introduction of FinTech has further accelerated this shift, making it possible for financial transactions to take place over digital trading platforms and across physical boundaries.

Yet, even as the emergence of globalisation and financialisation intuitively suggest the inevitable spatial decentralisation of economic processes and activities, the reality is that financial activities have, by and large, remained concentrated within a select group of global financial centres.[3] Economists have described this tendency for financial activities to coalesce around a physical location as 'agglomeration' or 'clustering'.[4] This proliferation of cross-border economic activity and transactions has given rise to "new geographies of centrality" that favours and emphasises specific configurations or networks of major global cities.[5]

The irony of centralisation amid globalisation and financialisation has not gone unnoticed. In fact, it presents a puzzle for scholars and analysts, and an opportunity for governments and policymakers of global cities.

This chapter will discuss such tendencies towards centralisation in global finance, and how these have contributed towards the emergence and development of major global financial cities such as Singapore. Furthermore, centralisation is not merely an economic concept; there are also political connotations to centralisation. Indeed, political centralisation *within* Singapore has also been instrumental in driving the city-state's emergence and growth as a financial centre, and consolidating its core identity as a global financial city.

Indeed, much of Singapore's efforts to become a major economic and financial hub in the world are driven by its coherent and consistent approach to financial sector governance and policy. Hence, while the advent of FinTech would suggest a shift in financial activity from physical locations to cyberspace, Singapore's efforts at developing a FinTech ecosystem has instead resulted in the city's emergence as a FinTech hub. In other words: more centralisation.

This chapter will unpack and discuss these various aspects and conceptions of centralisation.

Centre and Region

Thanks to globalisation and the emergence of advanced ICT and internet technologies, it is now possible to speak of a global economy that spans across national boundaries and enmeshes economic actors within relations of interdependency. Gone are the days where products are made, sold, and consumed within a particular country or locale. Indeed, tracking the journey of a product's creation, from design to production and finally to retail, would entail an arduous trek across the major production centres of the world.

As a consequence of this widespread economic globalisation, global supply chains have become dislocated across different locations, with firms situating different parts of their production processes in locations that provide the greatest cost savings or economic benefits. Nor is this phenomenon solely restricted to manufacturing. The services sector has also experienced a significant extent of dislocation, as is evident in the outsourcing of call centres, IT services, and even the analysis of x-ray and MRI scans to developing countries such as India or the Philippines.

Having emerged as a leading supply chain hub that hosts the operations of many multinational, regional, and local logistic firms (including 20 of the world's top 25 third-party logistics companies) Singapore is well acquainted with such dislocation and outsourcing of global production of goods and services.[6] Indeed, Singapore's current success as a major supply chain hub, trade entrepôt, and global financial centre derives directly from its ability to leverage on such dislocation of global production of goods and services by hosting important components of global supply chains and producing exportable services such as finance.

At the heart of this centrality within global flows of goods, services, and capital, lies Singapore's efforts at promoting regionalism. Singapore has, from its independence and separation from its natural hinterland of Malaysia, been cognisant of the need to position itself at the centre of global trade, to become, in the words of its first Foreign Minister S. Rajaratnam, a 'global city' that is capable of tapping on the rest of the world as its hinterland.[7] Notions of regional and global centrality have therefore always existed within Singapore's policy milieu and national psyche.

As a result of this perceived need for regional and global centrality, Singapore has deliberately supported, and often championed, institutions that could serve to liberalise global trade and foster closer regional ties. As a small open economy, Singapore has long recognised the importance of free trade and access to regional markets in its effort. Known as its 'regionalisation drive', such efforts have effectively situated Singapore at a "global–local nexus" of international flows of goods, capital, finance, people, and knowledge.[8] This regionalisation drive has taken both bilateral and multilateral approaches.

In terms of bilateral regionalisation, Singapore has established free trade agreements (FTAs) with a range of countries, including the US, China, India, Japan, Korea, New Zealand, Panama, Peru, Australia, Cost-Rica, and Jordan.[9] In addition, Singapore has concluded FTA negotiations with the EU and Turkey, although these have not been fully implemented. Not only have these bilateral FTAs contributed to trade expansion through the lowering or even abolishment of barriers to trade, they have also contributed to the fostering of closer bilateral diplomatic ties.

Aside from bilateral FTAs, Singapore has also participated actively in multilateral FTAs. These include the ASEAN FTA, ASEAN–Australia–New Zealand FTA, ASEAN–China FTA,

ASEAN–India FTA, ASEAN–Japan Comprehensive Economic Partnership, ASEAN–Korea FTA, Trans-Pacific Partnership (TPP), and Regional Comprehensive Economic Partnership (RCEP).[10] By participating in these multilateral FTAs, Singapore has managed to locate itself within a broader economic region.

The most crucial of these various multilateral FTAs is arguably the ASEAN FTA. Formed in on August 8, 1967, ASEAN was conceived as an institution that could foster closer cooperation among its members in the economic, social, cultural, technical, and educational fields, among others.[11] ASEAN efforts at regionalisation would subsequently expand to include other regional economic powers, culminating in 'ASEAN Plus One' FTAs, such as the ASEAN–China FTA or the ASEAN–Japan FTA, among others.

These would further be expanded to form more complex institutions, such as the 'ASEAN Plus Three' forum of the RCEP. Indeed, this growing role of ASEAN in regional forums has been described as 'ASEAN centrality', with the grouping playing a driving role in various comprehensive regional trade and security arrangements.[12] There are therefore two layers of centrality that must be addressed in understanding Singapore's economic centralisation.

First, ASEAN is emerging as the central actor in Asian regionalism. This is reflected by its driving role in the 'ASEAN Plus' family of FTAs, which have arguably expanded to include emerging institutions such as the RCEP and the Free Trade Area of the Asia Pacific (FTAAP). While the RCEP seeks to harmonise ASEAN's various bilateral FTAs in the region, the FTAAP aims to achieve the same for the broader Pacific Rim region.

Second, Singapore has established a position of centrality within ASEAN, particularly through its roles as major trading node and leading financial centre in the Southeast Asian region.[13] Due to its advanced levels of economic and technological development, Singapore has often been seen as the "natural leader of ASEAN" and the "financial, commercial and diplomatic centre of the region".[14] This further emphasizes

Singapore's position of centrality, both within the Southeast Asian region and, through the various ASEAN Plus frameworks, in Asia more generally.

Having established Singapore's centrality in the region, it is only natural to wonder — what are the economic benefits and implications of such economic centralisation as well as the regionalisation policies that have underpinned it? According to a report published by the Ministry of Trade and Industry, Singapore's domestic exports to an FTA partner tends to increase by 18% two years after the FTA has entered into force, and a further 16% in the third year.[15] There are therefore statistically significant positive benefits from entering into an FTA.

At a more granular level, World Bank data shows that Singapore's merchandise exports have risen from US$52.73 billion in 1990 to US$350.506 billion in 2015.[16] Fig. 4.1 shows the rapid increase in Singapore's merchandise exports between the years 1990 and 2015. In particular, there was a dramatic increase in merchandise exports between 1990 and 1995, which corresponds with the Economic Development Board's "Regionalisation 2000" drive that was unveiled in the 1990s.[17] The goal of this drive was successfully achieved, as the near two-fold increase in merchandise exports between 2000 and 2005 shows.

A similar picture can be found in Singapore's service exports data,[18] with service exports doubling between 1990 and 1995, 2000 and 2005, as well as 2005 and 2010. This is illustrated in Fig. 4.2.

Fig. 4.1: Merchandise Exports (in Current US$ Billion)

Merchandise Exports	1990	1995	2000	2005	2010	2015
Current US$ Billion	52.73	118.268	137.804	229.649	351.867	350.506

Adapted from World Bank (2016), "Trade".

Fig. 4.2: Service Exports (BOP, Current US$ Billion)

Merchandise Exports	1990	1995	2000	2005	2010	2015
Current US$ Billion	12.811	25.97	25.97	46.427	100.832	139.611

Adapted from World Bank (2016), "Services Exports".

The continued exponential expansion of service exports well into the 2000s stands in stark contrast to the relatively stagnant level of merchandise exports from 2010 onwards. This reflects ongoing structural shifts in Singapore's economy and the process of financialisation, as discussed in Chapter 3.

Regardless, Singapore's regionalisation drive is expected to continue yielding economic gains for the city-state. For instance, the ASEAN Economic Community (AEC), which was established in late 2015, is expected to give a 9.5% boost to Singapore's GDP by 2030.[19] Aside from expanding trade flows, the AEC is also expected to enhance cross-border flows of services and investment, driving up demand for financial products and services.[20] All these will contribute immensely to Singapore's position as a trade hub and a global financial centre.

As this section has shown, Singapore's development and continued success as a global financial centre is driven by its economic centrality within both ASEAN and the broader Asia Pacific region. This centrality was driven by the government's efforts at supporting and encouraging economic regionalisation. There is therefore another layer of centralisation that needs to be addressed — centralisation in Singapore's political and policy processes.

Politics and Governance

At the heart of Singapore's success as a thriving global financial centre is the active role of the government in implementing policies that support financial sector development and enforcing regulations that ensure financial market stability. Indeed, it has long been noted that factors associated with good governance, such as the rule of law, adept use of industrial policy, and strong stakeholder relations, have been instrumental in Singapore's financial sector development.[21] But which of these factors are unique to Singapore's historical and contextual background, and which of these are replicable by other countries?

An important consequence of globalisation, as well as the economic liberalisation and deregulation that have often followed the globalisation and opening up of a country's economy, is what urban scholar Saskia Sassen has described as a "partial unbundling or at least weakening of the nation as a spatial unit", and the ascendance of cities and regions as new spatial units and scales in the global system.[22] As a consequence, major cities, known as 'global cities' or 'world cities', have emerged to play an outsized role in the global economy,[23] at times even overshadowing state-centred institutions of global economic diplomacy.[24]

Furthermore, the continued participation of nation states in economic networks dominated by cities has resulted in a 'de-nationalisation' of certain components of the nation state.[25] A key example of this is the formation of 'free trade zones' — such as the one in Shanghai — where economic and regulatory policies are significantly more liberal and hence attractive to multinational firms and financial institutions.[26] Particularly popular in developing economies such as China, free trade zones (FTZ) are associated with a certain extent of policy and political decentralisation, hence granting the zone a measure of policy autonomy.[27]

By establishing such free trade zones, nation states are increasingly able to set aside a circumscribed geographical area that approximates the economic and regulatory conditions of a modern global city, even as economic and policy conditions in the rest of the country remain relatively unchanged. In the case of Shanghai, this included economic liberalisation within the FTZ, allowing foreign firms and institutions to operate within the zone, as well as allowing the sale of game consoles such as the PlayStation 4 or Xbox One, and granting greater access to online shopping platforms within the FTZ.[28]

Such free trade zones therefore allow for the artificial establishment of an urban centre that also serves as a point of connection with other global cities. As the saying goes, imitation is the best form of flattery. This prevalence of artificial economic urban zones in the form of free trade zones, along with the ongoing urbanisation drive among Asian economic powerhouses such as China and India, lends credence to the emergence and eventual dominance of the city as a major player in today's global political economy.

Given its unique position as one of the world's few functioning city-states, this growing role of the city in the global economy is especially pertinent to Singapore. Indeed, Olds and Yeung categorise Singapore as a 'global city-state', that, unlike other global cities, does not have an immediate hinterland within the same national territorial boundaries but rather, take a region or even other distant parts of the world as its hinterland.[29] An important advantage of being a global city-state derives from its ability and legitimacy to mobilise resources towards the achievement of national objectives, avoiding potential national-versus-urban politics that often arise in global cities situated within a national territory.[30]

There is, in other words, a significant extent of political centralisation within a global city-state that not only facilitates and expedites policymaking, but also elevates urban policies to the national level, imbuing what are otherwise municipal or local level policies with national level resources and legitimacy. Such political centralisation is particularly pronounced in Singapore, given its position as an independent city-state that enjoys complete autonomy and control over its defence and foreign policies. This is in contrast to Hong Kong, which possesses autonomy only in economic and social policies, with defence and diplomacy determined by the Chinese central government.

Indeed, Singapore's economic and financial sector policies are often intertwined with national security issues. For instance, Singapore's lack of natural resources and its perceived vulnerability continue to drive its efforts at ensuring economic growth and conducting economic diplomacy.[31] Furthermore, geopolitical instability, emerging national security challenges such as cyber-security, and a conscripted military force constrained by a small population all translate into a need for economic resources that can be used to maintain and technologically enable Singapore's military forces.[32]

The relationship between economic policy and national security can run both ways as well, with the maintenance of a sufficiently strong military force related to a need to ensure access to trade routes for Singapore's exports as well as crucial essential supplies such as water.[33] In short, there is a strong relationship between economic policy and national interests. This imbues economic development in Singapore with an urgency that is not necessarily present in other cities that exist as a component of a larger nation state.

This centralisation of economic and financial sector development is further compounded by the consolidation of political power and policy legitimacy in the ruling People's Action Party (PAP).[34] Having won every general election since independence, the PAP has established itself as the dominant centre of Singapore's politics and governance, and the key driving force for its economic policies.[35] The PAP's strength at the polls has given it a significant level of political legitimacy and policy autonomy. Furthermore, the PAP's political strength has also imbued it with a significant level of insulation from interest groups.

Indeed, Singapore's success as a financial centre has in part been attributed to the political will of its government in deciding to establish a financial sector, particularly at the early stages of its independence.[36]

However, the PAP's political legitimacy and policy autonomy can only be translated into effective policy outcomes through an effective public administration. As a proponent of the 'Asian Developmental State' model of economic development, Singapore's industrial and economic policies is typically led and driven by the Economic Development Board (EDB), which acts as the archetypical 'pilot agency'.[37] However, the need for specialised domain knowledge in managing and leading the financial services sector had led to the establishment of the Monetary Authority of Singapore (MAS) as the pilot or lead agency for financial sector development.[38]

This has significant implications for the MAS's organisational design. First, the MAS works closely with the government and is in fact housed within the Prime Minister's Office. This differs from most financial regulatory agencies, which are typically independent and operate at arm's length from the government of the day. Second, and in addition to its role as a regulator, the MAS is also tasked with developing and promoting Singapore's financial sector. Again, this is not typical of most financial regulatory agencies, which tend not to engage in promotional activities.

As such, there is a significant extent of centralisation in Singapore's governance and politics, with such political centralisation contributing immensely to the city's growth and development as a global financial centre. As a relatively small city-state, Singapore has never seen the need for the extensive administrative decentralisation and political devolution that other larger nation states have initiated over the years. However, the centralised nature of Singapore's political system and public administration has contributed to its bureaucratic efficiency and policy expediency.

A further implication of this is the government's ability to recognise emerging sectors or 'niches' and formulate the necessary policy initiatives for the development of these niches,[39] with a recent instance of this being Singapore's emerging FinTech sector. This is discussed in the next section.

Growing a FinTech Hub

Faced with sluggish regional and global growth as well as emerging competition from other financial centres, Singapore has identified FinTech as a potential growth sector, with the government aiming to transform the city-state into a global FinTech hub.[40] Indeed, the FinTech sector is becoming an increasingly crucial element of Singapore's unique proposition as a global financial centre, bringing forth both threats and opportunities for both the development and governance of Singapore's financial services industry.

On the one hand, FinTech poses a disruptive potential to traditional banking and finance, providing consumers with alternative means and sources of finance and capital allocation.[41] Such disruption could post significant headwinds for most global financial centres, which remain strongly focused on traditional banking and finance activities. However, and on the other hand, the emergence of FinTech has also brought forth new opportunities for banks and financial institutions that are willing and able to harness these new tools and technologies in their operations.

These dual dynamics — threat and opportunity — have prompted governments of major financial centres to pay closer attention to the burgeoning FinTech industry, in an attempt to address the emerging threats that FinTech may bring to traditional banking and finance and at the same time, explore any potential economic gains and opportunities that may emerge from this emerging sector. Given its strengths in banking, asset management and insurance, Singapore is not exempt from these pressures.

Deputy Prime Minister and Coordinating Minister for Economic and Social Policies Tharman Shanmugaratnam, who also serves as Chairman of the MAS, has noted in a speech that the ongoing growth and development of FinTech in Singapore will involve a "tension between new players and established players, or the tension between disruption of existing players and collaboration with them".[42] However, such tensions of disruption and collaboration are not necessarily new to Singapore, with the city hosting a wide array of international and domestic financial institutions of all shapes and sizes, collaborating and at the same time competing with each other.

Nonetheless, the benefits of FinTech are perceived to outweigh its costs or threats. This is evident in the government's decision and efforts to make Singapore a leading global FinTech hub. As noted in an *Economist* report, Singapore aims to develop a "thriving FinTech industry that supports, rather than undermines, incumbent big banks", with the MAS seeking to invest S$225 million in FinTech by 2020, and its Chief FinTech Officer Sopnendu Mohanty hoping to attract more 'enablers' than 'disrupters' in an effort to meld the value propositions of FinTech and mainstream banking.[43]

Indeed, such efforts to fold FinTech into the existing mix of financial activities is reminiscent of other earlier efforts to diversify Singapore's mix of financial activities, from the Asian Dollar Market to more recent efforts to establish the fund management, commodities and insurance markets. In all cases, the aim has been to create an integrated mix of financial activities, enhancing Singapore's attractiveness as a financial centre to a broader swath of investors and financiers.

As a consequence, banks have established asset management arms while fund managers and insurers have established tie-up promotions with banks in order to market their products to a broader audience. A similar process is already underway in FinTech. For instance, the Development Bank of Singapore (DBS) has engaged International Business Machines Corp. (IBM) for the use of its cognitive system Watson, which will allow the bank to analyse large volumes of data and provide more customised asset management services.[44] Both DBS and the Australia and New Zealand Banking Group (ANZ) have also recently established their individual FinTech innovation labs.[45]

The emergence of such industry collaborations and the establishment of new FinTech labs suggest the presence of a burgeoning ecosystem of FinTech innovators and consumers. Indeed, it has been noted that Singapore already possesses the three key elements of a successful FinTech ecosystem – the presence of FinTech start-ups and entrepreneurs, available investment capital to fund the growth of start-ups, and an educated community of experts and mentors.[46] As was the case with economic centralisation, Singapore is fast becoming a centralised hub of activity and investment in FinTech tools and start-ups.

Given its existing strength as a global financial centre, Singapore's burgeoning FinTech industry will likely cement its position as a hub for both mainstream finance and FinTech for the region. Indeed, observers expect Singapore to remain a leading FinTech hub, and a springboard into the ASEAN countries as well as the broader Asian region for the foreseeable future.[47] However, it is also important to note that Singapore's emergence as a FinTech hub is not entirely an organic process.

Similar to its earlier development as a financial hub, and as discussed in the earlier section on centralisation in politics and governance, Singapore's emerging role as a leading FinTech hub is driven by a raft of supporting policies. These include state investments, a light touch approach to regulating FinTech start-ups, and the establishment of a regulatory 'sandbox' that allows start-ups and financial institutions to test new FinTech products and innovations within a circumscribed space and duration, subject to regulatory safeguards that aim to contain any impacts of failure on the overall financial system.[48]

Along with the regulatory sandbox, the MAS has also established a FinTech Innovation Lab. Located within the MAS building, the Lab allows the MAS to experiment FinTech solutions with financial institutions and start-ups, facilitate consultation for start-ups with industry experts, as well as host training and networking activities for the FinTech community.[49] This establishment of a FinTech innovation lab by the MAS is in itself an instance of policy innovation, since most, if not all, FinTech innovation labs tend to be set up by and housed within private sector financial institutions.

In order to facilitate its FinTech-related policies and regulations, the MAS set up a FinTech and Innovation Group (FTIG) within its organisational structure on July 27, 2015. Led by the MAS's Chief FinTech Officer Sonendu Mohanty, the FTIG is responsible for both regulatory policies and the development of strategies related to the use of technology and innovation for managing risks, enhancing efficiency, and strengthening competitiveness in the financial services sector.[50]

As such, there are two processes of centralisation involved in Singapore's emergence as a FinTech hub. First, Singapore is becoming the leading FinTech hub for Southeast Asia and a forerunner in the broader Asian region. This is the result of its thriving FinTech ecosystem, which provides a centre around which FinTech entrepreneurs, start-ups, and investments converge. Secondly, the development and governance of the FinTech sector remains largely driven by the MAS, with the authority providing both regulatory and physical infrastructures in support of emerging FinTech start-ups.

Conclusion

As this chapter has discussed, a significant extent of economic and political/policy centralisation characterises Singapore's overall development as a global financial centre, with the city-state harnessing its centrality within regional and global economic activity, and the MAS playing a central role as both regulator and development agency for Singapore's financial services sector. Such economic and policy centralisation can be characterised roughly as external and internal centrality.

As discussed above, Singapore's emergence and rise as a global financial centre has depended on its ability to leverage upon the external economy and position itself as a regional and global hub for economic activity. Such economic centralisation therefore requires Singapore to achieve a significant extent of centrality within the regional and global economy. As a nation-state, Singapore has therefore attained centrality in its external environment.

This is complemented by the internal centrality of the government, especially with regards to the key role that the MAS plays in regulating and guiding the development of Singapore's financial services sector. Indeed, the MAS's position as the 'go-to' agency for all matters related to the financial sector has proven to be a key competitive advantage for Singapore, with financial institutions and banking sector executives often attributing Singapore's attractiveness as a financial centre to the accessibility of the MAS's regulatory officials.[51]

Like globalisation and financialisation, centralisation is a major driving force behind Singapore's success as a global financial centre. More precisely, it is Singapore's ability to harness the economic, political, and technological aspects of centralisation that has cemented its position as a regional and global hub for financial activity and more recently, FinTech. However, the three processes discussed in this book so far — globalisation, financialisation, and centralisation — do not operate independently of each other. As the next chapter will discuss, they are interdependent and mutually reinforcing.

Endnote

1. Kenichi Ohmae, *The Borderless World, Rev Ed: Power and Strategy in the Interlinked Economy*, Revised ed. (New York: HarperBusiness, 1999).
2. Thomas L. Friedman, *The World Is Flat: A Brief History of the Twenty-First Century*, 1st ed. (New York: Farrar, Straus and Giroux, 2005).
3. Saskia J. Sassen, *Cities in a World Economy*, 4th ed. (California: SAGE Publications, Inc, 2011).
4. E.P. Davis, "International Financial Centres — An Industrial Analysis," Bank of England Discussion Paper, (September 1990); Thomas Gehrig, "Cities and the Geography of Financial Centers," in *Economies of Cities: Theoretical Perspectives*, ed. Jean-Marie Huriot and Jacques-Francois Thiesse (Cambridge: Cambridge University Press, 2000), pp. 415–446.
5. Saskia J. Sassen, *Global Networks, Linked Cities* (New York, NY, 10001: Routledge, 2001), p. 2.
6. Kelvin Wong, "Differentiate Your Business Through Supply Chain Optimisation," *Singapore Economic Development Board*, June 5, 2015,/content/edb/en/resources/downloads/articles/supply-chain-optimisation.html.
7. S. Rajaratnam, "'Global City' Success for S'pore: Raja," *The Straits Times*, February 7, 1972.
8. Brenda Yeoh and Katie Willis, "The Global-Local Nexus: Singapore's Regionalisation Drive," *Geography* 82, No. 2 (1997): 183; Karen P.Y. Lai, "Singapore's Economic Landscapes: Local Transformations and Global Networks," in *Changing Landscapes of Singapore: Old Tensions, New Discoveries*, ed. Elaine Lynn-Ee Ho, Yuan Woon Chih, and Kamalini Ramdas (Singapore: NUS Press, 2013), pp. 196–217.
9. International Enterprise Singapore, "Singapore FTAs — Trade from Singapore," 2016, http://www.iesingapore.gov.sg/Trade-From-Singapore/International-Agreements/free-trade-agreements/Singapore-FTA.

10. *Ibid.*
11. ASEAN, "History," ASEAN Website, *ASEAN/ONE VISION ONE IDENTITY ONE COMMUNITY*, (2016), http://asean.org/asean/about-asean/history/.
12. Mark Rolls, "Centrality and Continuity: ASEAN and Regional Security since 1967," *East Asia* 29, No. 2 (June 1, 2012): 127–139, doi:10.1007/s12140-011-9160-1; Mely Caballero-Anthony, "Understanding ASEAN's Centrality: Bases and Prospects in an Evolving Regional Architecture," *The Pacific Review* 27, No. 4 (August 8, 2014): 563–584, doi:10.1080/09512748.2014.924227.
13. J. J. Woo, *Business and Politics in Asia's Key Financial Centres — Hong Kong, Singapore and Shanghai*, 1st ed. (Singapore: Springer, 2016); J.J. Woo, *Singapore as an International Financial Centre: History, Politics and Policy* (London: Palgrave Macmillan, 2016).
14. Simon Shen, "Why Singapore Plays a Pivotal Role in ASEAN," *EJ Insight*, April 20, 2015, http://www.ejinsight.com/20150420-singapore-pivotal-role-asean/.
15. Ministry of Trade and Industry, "Do Free Trade Agreements Matter? Evaluating the Impact of FTAs on Singapore's Domestic Exports of Goods," Feature Article (Singapore: Ministry of Trade and Industry, 2011).
16. World Bank, "Trade," 2016, http://data.worldbank.org/topic/trade?locations=SG.
17. Dimitrios Konstadakopulos, *Learning for Innovation in the Global Knowledge Economy: A European and South-East Asian Perspective* (Bristol, U.K.: Intellect Books, 2004); Alexius Pereira, "Singapore's Regionalization Strategy," *Journal of the Asia Pacific Economy* 10, No. 3 (January 1, 2005): 380–396, doi:10.1080/13547860500163480.
18. World Bank, "Service Exports," *World Bank Database*, 2016, http://data.worldbank.org/indicator/BX.GSR.NFSV.CD?locations=SG.
19. Jeremy Koh, "New Asean Economic Community could give Singapore GDP a 9.5% boost by 2030: HSBC," *The Straits Times*, November 23, 2015, http://www.straitstimes.com/business/economy/new-asean-economic-community-could-give-singapore-gdp-a-95-boost-by-2030-hsbc.
20. *Ibid.*
21. J. J. Woo, "Beyond the Neoliberal Orthodoxy: Alternative Financial Policy Regimes in Asia's Financial Centres," *Critical Policy Studies* 9, No. 3 (2015): 297–316; Jiangyu Wang, "The Rise of Singapore as International Financial Centre: Political Will, Industrial Policy, and Rule of Law," in *Finance, Rule of Law and Development in Asia*, ed. Jiaxin Hu, Matthias Vanhullebusch, and Andrew Harding (Leiden: Brill Nijhoff, 2016), pp. 1–17, http://booksandjournals.brillonline.com/content/books/b9789004315815_002; J. J. Woo, *Business and Politics in Asia's Key Financial Centres — Hong Kong, Singapore and Shanghai*; Woo, *Singapore as an International Financial Centre: History, Politics and Policy*.
22. Saskia J. Sassen, *Global Networks, Linked Cities*, p. 1.
23. Peter Geoffrey Hall, *The World Cities* (New York: McGraw-Hill, 1966); Saskia J. Sassen, *The Global City: New York, London, Tokyo.*, 2nd ed. (Princeton, N.J: Princeton University

Press, 2001); John Friedman, "The World City Hypothesis," in *The City: The City in Global Context*, ed. Michael Pacione (London: Routledge, 2002), pp. 151–163.

24. Jun Jie Woo and Debbie Loo, "Sharing Solutions City-to-City," *TODAY*, May 29, 2014, http://www.todayonline.com/singapore/sharing-solutions-city-city.
25. Saskia J. Sassen, *De-Nationalization* (Princeton, N.J.: Princeton University Press, 2003); Saskia Sassen, *Territory, Authority, Rights: From Medieval to Global Assemblages*, Updated ed. (Princeton, N.J.: Princeton University Press, 2008).
26. Jun Jie Woo, "Free Trade Zone Fits into Shanghai's Financial Ambition," *South China Morning Post*, July 20, 2013; Giovanni Palmioli and Adam Heal, "Structural Economic Reform in China: The Role of the Shanghai Free Trade Zone," Trade Insights (Washington, D.C.: UNESCAP, November 2014); Zheng Wan *et al.*, "Policy and Politics behind Shanghai's Free Trade Zone Program," *Journal of Transport Geography* 34 (January 2014): 1–6, doi:10.1016/j.jtrangeo.2013.10.015.
27. Jing Ye, "Decentralized Authorities and Transnational Policy Diffusion: The Case of Free Trade Zone in China," *World Economics and Policy*, No. 7 (2014), http://en.cnki.com.cn/Article_en/CJFDTotal-SJJZ201407009.htm.
28. Beijing Review, "Shanghai FTZ: One Year On — Beijing Review," *Beijing Review*, 2016, http://www.bjreview.com.cn/Cover_Stories_Series_2014/shanghai_ftz_one_year_on.html.
29. Kris Olds and Henry Yeung, "Pathways to Global City Formation: A View from the Developmental City-State of Singapore," *Review of International Political Economy* 11, No. 3 (June 1, 2004): 507, doi:10.1080/0969229042000252873.
30. *Ibid*, p. 508.
31. Michael Leifer, *Singapore's Foreign Policy: Coping with Vulnerability* (London: Routledge, 2000); Linda Low, *The Political Economy of a City-State: Government-Made Singapore* (Oxford: Oxford University Press, 2001).
32. Ryo Hinata-Yamaguchi, "Singapore's Military Modernization," *The Diplomat*, April 27, 2012, http://thediplomat.com/2012/04/singapores-military-modernization/; Franz-Stefan Gady, "Singapore's Defense Budget Climbs 5.7 Percent," *The Diplomat*, March 19, 2015, http://thediplomat.com/2015/03/singapores-defense-budget-climbs-5-7-percent/.
33. Dhara Ranasinghe, "Singapore, the Tiny State with Military Clout," *CNBC*, February 9, 2014, http://www.cnbc.com/2014/02/07/singapore-the-tiny-state-with-military-clout.html.
34. Diane K. Mauzy and R. S. Milne, *Singapore Politics Under the People's Action Party*, 1st ed. (London ; New York: Routledge, 2002); Bilveer Singh, *Politics and Governance in Singapore: An Introduction*, 2nd ed. (Singapore: McGraw-Hill Education (Asia), 2012); Kenneth Paul Tan, "The Singapore Parliament: Representation, Effectiveness, and Control," in *Parliaments in Asia: Institutional Building and Political Development*, ed. Yongnian Zheng, Liang Fook Lye, and Wilheim Hofmeister (Oxford, U.K.: Routledge, 2013), pp. 27–46, https://www.academia.edu/5057723/Tan_Kenneth_Paul_The_Singapore_parliament_representation_effectiveness_and_control_._In_Parliaments_in_Asia_Institutional_Building_and_Political_Development_ed._Zheng_Yongnian_Lye_Liang_Fook_and_Wilhelm_Hofmeister._Oxford_Routledge_2013.

35. Low, *The Political Economy of a City-State*; Linda Low, *The Political Economy of a City-State Revised* (Singapore: Marshall Cavendish, 2006).
36. Wang, *The Rise of Singapore as International Financial Centre.*
37. W. G. Huff, "The Developmental State, Government, and Singapore's Economic Development since 1960," *World Development* 23, No. 8 (August 1995): 1421–1438; Martin Perry, *Singapore: A Developmental City State* (Chichester: Wiley, 1997); Linda Low, "The Singapore Developmental State in the New Economy and Polity," *The Pacific Review* 14, No. 3 (January 1, 2001): 411–441.
38. J. J. Woo, *Singapore as an International Financial Centre: History, Politics and Policy.*
39. J. J. Woo, *Business and Politics in Asia's Key Financial Centres — Hong Kong, Singapore and Shanghai*; Woo, *Singapore as an International Financial Centre: History, Politics and Policy.*
40. The Economist, "Singapore Tries to Become a Fintech Hub," *The Economist*, January 14, 2017, http://www.economist.com/news/finance-and-economics/21714384-city-state-wants-fintech-bolsters-not-disrupts-mainstream; Saeed Azhar and Marius Zaharia, "In Race to Be Asia's Fintech Hub, Singapore Leads Hong Kong," *Reuters*, July 3, 2016, http://www.reuters.com/article/us-singapore-fintech-idUSKCN0ZJ10P.
41. Citi, "Digital Disruption: How FinTech Is Forcing Banks to a Tipping Point," Citi GPS: Global Perspectives & Solutions (New York, N.Y.: Citigroup, March 2016).
42. Tharman Shanmugaratnam, "Speech at the Launch of the Singapore FinTech Festival" (Speech, Launch of the Singapore FinTech Festival at the Asia Society, New York, N.Y., April 12, 2016), http://www.mas.gov.sg/News-and-Publications/Speeches-and-Monetary-Policy-Statements/Speeches/2016/Speech-at-the-Launch-of-the-Singapore-FinTech-Festival.aspx.
43. *The Economist*, "Singapore Tries to Become a Fintech Hub."
44. Alex Barinka, "IBM's Watson to Help Rich DBS Clients with 'Jeopardy' Smarts," *Bloomberg.com*, January 9, 2014, https://www.bloomberg.com/news/articles/2014-01-09/ibm-carves-out-1-billion-new-unit-for-jeopardy-champ-watson.
45. Finextra, "ANZ and DBS Open New Labs to Coincide with Singapore Fintech Festival," *Finextra Research*, November 14, 2016, https://www.finextra.com/newsarticle/29756/anz-and-dbs-open-new-labs-to-coincide-with-singapore-fintech-festival.
46. Markus Gnirck and Gerben Visser, "Singapore, the FinTech Hub for Southeast Asia," in *The FinTech Book*, ed. Susanne Chishti and Janos Barberis (John Wiley & Sons, Ltd, 2016), pp. 58–60, http://onlinelibrary.wiley.com/doi/10.1002/9781119218906.ch16/summary.
47. *Ibid.*
48. Azhar and Zaharia, "In Race to Be Asia's Fintech Hub, Singapore Leads Hong Kong"; Monetary Authority of Singapore, "MAS FinTech Regulatory Sandbox," *MAS Website*, November 26, 2016, http://www.mas.gov.sg/Singapore-Financial-Centre/Smart-Financial-Centre/FinTech-Regulatory-Sandbox.aspx; The Economist, "Singapore Tries to Become a Fintech Hub."

49. Monetary Authority of Singapore, "MAS Establishes FinTech Innovation Lab," Press Release (Singapore: Monetary Authority of Singapore, August 24, 2016), http://www.mas.gov.sg/News-and-Publications/Media-Releases/2016/MAS-establishes-FinTech-Innovation-Lab.aspx.
50. Monetary Authority of Singapore, "MAS Sets up New FinTech and Innovation Group," *MAS Website*, November 26, 2016, http://www.mas.gov.sg/news-and-publications/media-releases/2015/mas-sets-up-new-fintech-and-innovation-group.aspx.
51. Kam-Hon Lee and Ilan Vertinsky, "Strategic Adjustment of International Financial Centres (IFCs) in Small Economies: A Comparative Study of Hong Kong and Singapore," *Journal of Business Administration* 17, No. 1–2 (1988): 151–172; J. J. Woo, *Business and Politics in Asia's Key Financial Centres — Hong Kong, Singapore and Shanghai*; J. J. Woo, *Singapore as an International Financial Centre: History, Politics and Policy.*

TO VIEW THE WORLD SUB SPECIE AETERNI IS TO VIEW IT AS A WHOLE — A LIMITED WHOLE. FEELING THE WORLD AS A LIMITED WHOLE — IT IS THIS THAT IS MYSTICAL.

LUDWIG WITTGENSTEIN
TRACTATUS LOGICO-PHILOSOPHICUS
6.45

CHAPTER FIVE

Conclusion

Global financial centres have long been subjects of academic inquiry and public discourse, with governments aiming to transform their cities into thriving financial centres, citizens vying for employment within them, and scholars seeking to understand the factors and forces that have contributed to the success of specific financial centres. However, these efforts and discourses have tended to take the global financial centre as a single unit of analysis. What has emerged is therefore a monolithic and unnaturally unified concept of a Global Financial Centre, with its constituent parts undifferentiated from the whole.

Yet we know that global financial centres, being products of human endeavour and loci of socioeconomic interactions, are, in reality, complex entities made up of a messy mix of people, businesses, and governments. Evidence of this can be found in the mid-day crowds of central Hong Kong or the rush hour traffic in Singapore's central business district. The reality is that global financial centres are much more than skyscrapers and infrastructure; they are also spaces of social, economic, and political interactions. This also means that global financial centres are driven by social, economic, and political processes, with these processes converging to finally form the image and construct of a global financial centre.

In taking the global financial centre as conceptually given, we tend to neglect the presence of these diverse processes and the ways in which they culminate in a city's successful transformation into a global financial centre. In focusing on the final outcome (a successful financial centre) rather than the processes that have led to this outcome, analysts have not only placed the cart before the horse, but entirely forgotten about the horse itself. There is therefore a need to place greater attention on the interdependent forces that have driven the emergence and success of a global financial centre.

This book has sought to do so by disaggregating the concept of a global financial centre into three distinct but interrelated processes — globalisation, financialisation, and centralisation. All three processes have been the subject of much study and research in the fields of economics and political science, with this existing body of work providing the basis of this book's analysis. More importantly for the purposes of this book, these three processes correspond neatly with the three core identities of a global financial centre:

- Its role in facilitating global flows of capital, people, and power.
- Its simultaneous dependence on and support for processes of financialisation.
- Its position as a hub around which financial institutions and financial activities converge.

In fact, one could make the argument that a global financial centre would lose its ontological and existential basis — its *raison d'être* — if any one of these three identities and their corresponding processes were to somehow become omitted. Hence, the three processes identified in this book are not only driving forces behind Singapore's emergence and subsequent success as a global financial centre, they are also defining features of the city-state's position as a leading financial hub.

Furthermore, these three processes tend to take effect in and are hence mediated through the realms of economics, politics, and technology. Hence, for instance, while globalisation gives rise to important economic, political, and technological implications, it can also be somewhat driven by factors and forces within one or more of these three realms. Naturally, the same can be said for financialisation and centralisation as well. This array of processes, forces, and implications are illustrated in Fig. 5.1 below.

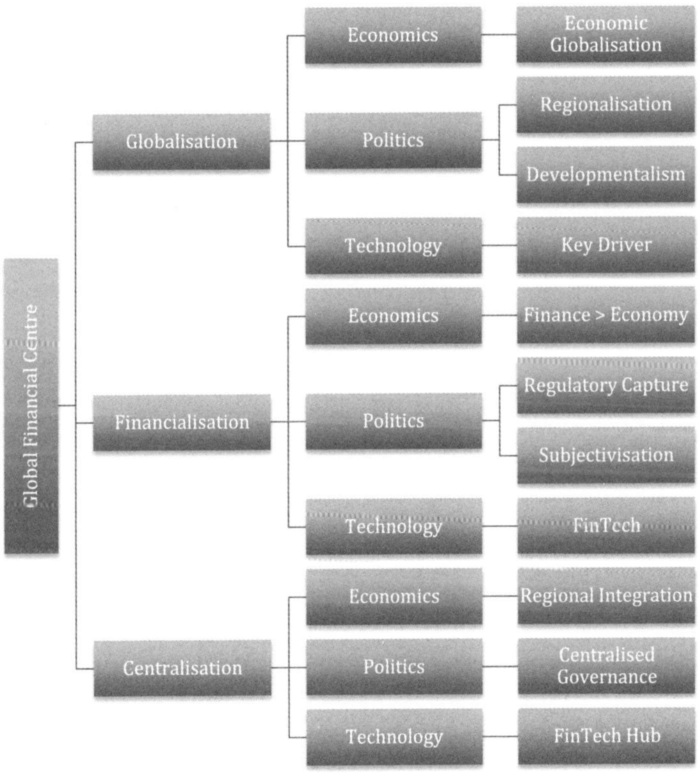

Fig. 5.1: Three Processes of a Global Financial Centre

While it is neither helpful nor feasible to provide a complete explication of the various processes and forces illustrated in Fig. 5.1 above,[a] a few points are nonetheless worth reiterating.

[a] For an in-depth discussion of each process, please refer to Chapters 2 to 4.

Despite its relatively longer history,[1] globalisation remains imbued with a significant extent of complexity and unpredictability. While economic globalisation is relatively unproblematic, emphasising the key economic drivers of globalisation such as global trade and economic liberalisation, the impact of globalisation in the political realm has been less clear-cut, with states seeking to extend their economic reach through regionalisation but yet retaining a significant extent of control over domestic economic development through a continued adherence to developmentalism. Furthermore, such efforts at regionalisation and developmentalism are not simply a result of globalisation; they often stimulate further globalisation.

Similarly, while technology has proven to be a key driver of globalisation (especially in terms of ICT and transport technologies), it is also dependent on these forces of globalisation for its continued development and proliferation. What has therefore emerged is a mixed picture of the ways in which globalisation impact the development of a global financial centre, with causality between globalisation and driving forces at times running both ways and often in a non-linear manner.

In contrast, financialisation has proven to be more pervasive and clear-cut in its impacts. In the realm of the economy, financialisation has resulted in the proliferation of financial activities and actors, often at the detriment of real economic activity. As a consequence, the financial services sector is beginning to replace real economic activities, such as trade and manufacturing, as both a driver of economic growth and source of employment. Similarly, financialisation has begun to reshape the political landscape, at both the state and individual levels.

At the level of the state, the growth of the financial services sector has led to the emergence of financial institutions as influential political actors, with their economic clout lending weight to their ability to lobby policymakers. In some jurisdictions, this has led to what is known as 'regulatory capture', with New York and London being cases in point.[2]

At the individual level, financialisation has driven the process of financial subjectivisation, with the social interactions and identities of individual citizens often defined in terms of and animated by the inherent logics and incentives of finance.

This pervasiveness of finance in the sociopolitical sphere is further accelerated by the permeation of finance in the realm of technology, with the result being what is known as 'FinTech', which simply put, is the application of technological tools and innovations to financial transactions and processes. More importantly, the emergence of FinTech has revealed potential economic gains from such applications of technology to finance and new business models for achieving these gains. While these new business models are placing competitive pressure on traditional mainstream banking and finance, the disruptive nature of FinTech has not gone unnoticed by governments either.

Indeed, FinTech has become an increasingly crucial element of a 21st century global financial centre. Given its disruptive nature and economic potential, governments of major financial centres are aiming to augment their existing financial sectors with FinTech. Like most other financial services, this often requires ensuring a city's attractiveness as a hub of FinTech activity and investments. This growing interest in developing FinTech hubs relates to the third major process discussed in this book — centralisation.

Indeed, the emergence of FinTech hubs reflects growing centralisation in technology, with FinTech start-ups and entrepreneurs gravitating towards specific cities or locations with the necessary supporting infrastructure. More often than not, such cities are already thriving financial hubs that have already experienced a significant extent of economic centralisation. As Chapter 4 has discussed, such economic centralisation is often strongly associated with processes of regional integration, with financial hubs emerging from cities that have established a significant level of centrality within their immediate regions.

The establishment of such economic and technological centrality, especially among Asian cities that have experienced an accelerated rate of development, is typically driven by centrality within the city's governance and policy processes. There are two aspects to such centralised governance. First, centralised governance often involves a coherent and consolidated policy process. This is not difficult to achieve, especially at the relatively small scale of the city or municipality. A second element of centralisation in governance involves the presence of a strong government possessing a high level of political legitimacy.

In functioning democracies, this often requires achieving a majority in legislative bodies, which in turn expedites policymaking and legislation. All three processes, with their economic, political, and technological aspects, have played crucial roles in Singapore's success as a global financial centre. This is evident in the highly globalised and financialised state of its economy as well as its external centrality as a global financial hub and its internal centrality of policy and political coherence. However, not all of the dynamics discussed above are relevant to Singapore.

For instance, and as Chapter 3 has shown, Singapore remains relatively free from regulatory capture. This is largely due to the government's insulation from interest and lobby groups as well as the MAS's organisational firewalls that separates its regulatory and developmental functions. Regardless, the three processes of globalisation, financialisation, and centralisation — or more precisely, Singapore's ability to leverage on and harness these three processes — have contributed immensely to the city-state's transformation into a leading global financial centre, and more recently, its emergence as a FinTech hub.

However, and as some of the earlier discussions presented in this book have pointed out, the individual impacts of the three processes tend to be less than clear-cut or distinguishable from each other. Rather, the three processes are intertwined and can either operate in a complementary manner or give rise to conflicting interests and dynamics. There is therefore a need to think of the three processes in a more integrated manner.

Integrated Processes

Just as it is a hub around which money, people, and interests converge, a global financial centre can also be thought of as a confluence of processes, both material and ideational. This is, intuitively at least, already obvious in its etymology, with the term 'global financial centre' itself representative of the three processes of globalisation, financialisation, and centralisation. There are a variety of ways in which the three processes are intertwined and intermingled, with a significant level of complexity involved.

It is not the aim of this chapter to provide an exhaustive account of these. Instead, a broad discussion of the ways in which three processes are intertwined and hence impact or influence one another will be provided.

As the conceptually broadest and most pervasive of the three, globalisation has long been a key driving mechanism for both financialisation and centralisation. Specifically, globalisation has given rise to high degree of interconnectivity among states. This has in turn established the incentives and imperatives for the creation of economic and financial hubs that can leverage on this global interconnectivity to drive economic growth and development, i.e., economic centralisation.

Indeed, the very emergence of global financial centres has been associated with the increasing pre-eminence of a set of 'global cities' that act as 'command and control' centres in the global economy.[3] Furthermore, the speed and intensity at which financial institutions and their services have entered many of the world's major economies has depended upon the economic liberalisation and uninhibited (or at least less inhibited) movements of people and capital that are typically associated with globalisation.

These factors, economic liberalisation and greater mobility, have also allowed key cities to emerge as centralised hubs of economic and financial activity. While globalisation may well have replaced spatial constraints with heightened mobility and hence given rise to a 'borderless economy' that facilitates the seamless conduct of business across national boundaries,[4] it has also paradoxically favoured cities that possess the infrastructure or 'advanced producer services' necessary for sustaining the headquarters and command functions of global multinational corporations.[5]

Hence, while the economic and technological elements of globalisation have provided the means for the de-spatialisation and de-territorialisation of economic activity, it has also resulted in a greater need for centralised control of spatially dispersed economic activity. Indeed, central coordination of spatially dispersed economic activity is itself possible only with the advent of advanced ICT tools such as the internet. Such central coordination in turn depends on the presence of a pool of highly skilled workers and the availability of supporting infrastructure and services (such as accounting and legal services).[6]

As such, globalisation has given rise to the emergence of key urban nodes in the global political economy, with such nodes typically serving the multiple functions of global financial centre, international business and logistic hub, and maritime port city, among others. Indeed, the expanded flows of people, capital and ideas that have been associated with globalisation have only served to reiterate an ever-greater need for the efficient allocation of capital and resources across borders (i.e., financial markets) and locations from which firms can coordinate their global functions and activities (i.e., centralised hubs).

However, the relationship can also run counter, with centralisation and financialisation, once entrenched, serving to drive and reify the forces and processes of globalisation.

For instance, the widespread financialisation of many of the world's economies has served to further enmesh many of these economies within an interconnected and interdependent web of financial relations. This has both positive and negative implications, with such highly interconnected financial centres benefiting from the growing demand for financial services among other thriving financial centres but yet, at the same time, susceptible to financial contagion. As the GFC has shown, even financial centres that were financially sound, such as Singapore, could be susceptible to contagion effects.[7]

Either ways, financialisation has only served to strengthen linkages between cities and nations by expanding financial transactions and hence, deepening economic interdependency among them. Similarly, the emergence of centralised hubs and nodes of economic activity has served as a catalyst and lubricant for further economic globalisation, with global economic activity facilitated by the increasingly efficient ways in which firms are able to coordinate their increasingly dispersed global supply chains. The centralisation of economic activity in major global cities has, in other words, allowed for even greater de-territorialisation of economic activity.

Lastly, financialisation and centralisation are highly interconnected, as is evidenced by the continued growth of major global financial centres such as New York, London and Singapore, as well as the emergence of new financial centres such as Abu Dhabi, Shenzhen, and Shanghai. Certainly, the allure of a global financial centre is not lost on many of the governments of today's major cities, many of whom are seeking to transform their cities into leading global financial centres.

While FinTech and electronic trading have shifted financial transactions from the physical realm to cyberspace, it has in no way reduced the need for the face-to-face interactions that have been so crucial in the development of many of the world's major financial centres. Indeed, interpersonal proximity remains important in many global financial centres, as is evident in the spatial clustering of financial institutions within the city centre or the prevalence of FinTech 'clusters'.[8] Indeed, financial services and innovation remain highly dependent on physical proximity and interpersonal interactions, not only among firms, but among firms and policymakers as well.[9]

Singapore: A 3-in-1 Global Financial Centre

Globalisation, financialisation, and centralisation operate as highly intertwined and interdependent processes that drive the development of a global financial centre, with the extent and pervasiveness of these processes often determining a financial centre's success. As a major hub of global economic and financial activity, Singapore has similarly benefited from a convergence of these three processes, by supplementing its central geographical location in Asia with adroit industrial planning and economic policymaking.[10]

Hence, while many existing studies of Singapore's development as a global financial centre have tended to treat these three processes separately, for instance, by focusing on the global forces that have driven financial sector development or the urban aspects of financial sector development, the far messier reality is that globalisation, financialisation, and centralisation have all played co-equal roles in driving Singapore's development as a financial centre, with each process intermingling and interdependent.

Rather than a singular narrative, Singapore's development as a global financial centre can be better characterised as a '3-in-1' process, with globalisation, financialisation, and centralisation converging, intermingling, and finally manifest in the spatial, conceptual, and political–economic reality of the financial centre. Just like the 3-in-1 coffee mix that is such a ubiquitous feature of many Singaporean supermarkets, the individual ingredients of Singapore's success as a global financial centre are not necessarily distinguishable from each other.

Indeed, Singapore's historical development and current success as a leading global financial centre remains a product of this messy '3-in-1' reality of intermingled and interdependent processes. This suggests a rethink of the way cities and financial centres are conceived and governed. Rather than focusing on one singular facet of a financial centre, whether economic, urban, political, cultural, etc., there is a need to take an integrative and comprehensive approach to understanding global financial centres. Such a need is even more urgent, with the growing policy complexity that Singapore and many other cities are facing.[11]

From a policy perspective, this means that policymakers and political leaders will need to be comfortable with an ever greater extent of complexity and messiness in their policy processes and environs, as they seek to understand and navigate these highly intermingled and intertwined socioeconomic–political processes that continue to impact and influence the social, economic, and political development of the cities and nations that they govern. Navigating such policy complexity will in turn require certain skills or capacities among policymakers and leaders of global financial centres.

Much has been said about such capacities, often termed 'policy capacity', in the existing literature,[12] and it is well beyond the scope of this book to provide a comprehensive discussion of these. A few points, nonetheless, are worth including in our discussions here. First, it is important to consider the multi-faceted nature of policy capacity, with analytical, operational, and political capacities instrumental in ensuring effective financial governance.[13] Indeed, political capacities related to the management of stakeholders and industry actors are particularly important for governments seeking to manage an increasingly diverse financial ecosystem.[14]

Furthermore, growing policy complexity also suggests a heightened need for governments to ensure systemic stability in their cities and financial markets. This means a need to ensure greater resilience and robustness in policy processes, with the former often associated with ensuring a society's ability to 'bounce back' from any sudden changes or shocks and the former relating to a society's ability to continue functioning amid episodes of crisis and shock.[15] In either case, the ability of a global financial centre to sustain itself, and even thrive, amid complexity depends upon the level and quality of policy capacity among its policymakers.

Such capacity will also allow policymakers to identify emerging global trends and forces, such as the three processes of globalisation, financialisation, centralisation, and to be able to navigate these effectively. Taking an integrative '3-in-1' approach to financial governance therefore requires governments to build up a broad range of policy capacities, with analytical capacities facilitating the identification and recognition of emerging trends, operational capacities necessary for formulating and implementing the appropriate policy measures, and political capacities ensuring the legitimacy of these measures as well as building up social trust among citizens.

Future Trajectories and Final Thoughts

As the discussion above makes clear, more work needs to be done, not only in order to understand the ways in which major social, economic, and political forces impact the development of global financial centres such as Singapore, but also to delineate the various capacities and means with which policymakers can use to address these forces and direct them towards financial sector development. While this book has discussed the former, the latter will require further research.

Having discussed Singapore's development as a global financial centre, and the ways in which globalisation, financialisation, and centralisation have driven this development, it is only appropriate that we cast our eyes to the future. Having established its current position as a global hub for banking and finance, what do emerging trends in global financial markets portend for Singapore? How will Singapore adapt and adjust to these emerging trends, and through what means?

Firstly, the emergence of FinTech both as a potential force of disruption and a growing industry has given rise to a growing desire among the city-state's leaders and policymakers to establish Singapore as a premier FinTech hub. Various policy measures have already been put in place in order to achieve this, with the most significant of these being the FinTech innovation hub and regulatory sandbox. Given these measures, the government's continued interest in growing the FinTech industry, and the lack of a credible regional competitor, it is almost certain that Singapore will establish itself as a leading FinTech hub.

However, the growth of the FinTech industry does not necessarily come at the obsolescence of mainstream banking and finance. Rather, and as earlier discussions have shown, Singapore aims to integrate its burgeoning FinTech industry with its traditional strengths in mainstream banking and finance, insurance, and asset management. This means that Singapore's financial services sector will become increasingly diverse, featuring a diverse mix of banks, insurers, asset managers, and FinTech start-ups.

In other words, Singapore's future as a global financial centre is more akin to a 'Jack of all trades' rather than a 'one-trick pony'. Given the increasingly keen competition that the city-state faces, such diversity in financial services is necessary for Singapore's future success and relevance as a multifaceted and multidimensional financial centre. Indeed, diversity and multidimensionality will be crucial for financial centres seeking to ensure a thriving financial ecosystem and, at the same time, hedge against the threat of disruption and obsolescence that new financial innovations tend to bring.

An important consequence of such multidimensionality is a corresponding need for adaptability and diverse skill sets among both policymakers and financial sector professionals alike. With the rise of FinTech, a certain level of proficiency in managing and interpreting data will be increasingly crucial for both policymakers and financiers. While the government has made strong strides in growing such proficiencies, especially through its SkillsFuture programme, there remains a need to develop greater breadth and cross-functionality among policymakers and citizens, in order that they may function and thrive amid a '3-in-1' reality of intermingled policy processes.

Endnotes

1. Research and discourse on globalisation have arguably been in existence since the advent of global trade, although the coining of the term, its current conceptual form, and its implications cities, societies and polities are of a more recent vintage. For instance, see Saskia J. Sassen, "Whose City Is It? Globalization and the Formation of New Claims," *Public Culture* 8, No. 2 (1996): 205–223; Kenichi Ohmae, *The Borderless World, Rev Ed: Power and Strategy in the Interlinked Economy*, Revised ed. (New York: HarperBusiness, 1999); John W. Meyer, "Globalization Sources and Effects on National States and Societies," *International Sociology* 15, No. 2 (June 1, 2000): 233–248, doi:10.1177/0268580900015002006; Daniel W. Drezner, "Globalization and Policy Convergence," *International Studies Review* 3, No. 1 (January 1, 2001): 53–78; Kevin H. O'Rourke and Jeffrey G. Williamson, "When Did Globalisation Begin?," *European Review of Economic History* 6, No. 1 (April 1, 2002): 23–50, doi:10.1017/S1361491602000023; Joseph E. Stiglitz, *Globalization and Its Discontents* (New York: W.W. Norton, 2003); Martin Wolf, *Why Globalization Works*, 2nd ed. (New Haven: Yale University Press, 2005); Francis Fukuyama, *State-Building: Governance and World Order in the 21st Century* (Ithaca, N.Y: Cornell University Press, 2004); Joseph E. Stiglitz, *Making Globalization Work*, Reprint ed., (New York: W. W. Norton & Company, 2007); Dani Rodrik, *The Globalization Paradox: Democracy and the Future of the World Economy*, Reprint ed. (New York; London: W. W. Norton & Company, 2012).
2. Andrew Baker, "Restraining Regulatory Capture? Anglo-America, Crisis Politics and Trajectories of Change in Global Financial Governance," *International Affairs* 86, No. 3 (2010): 647–663.
3. Saskia J. Sassen, *Cities in a World Economy*, 4th ed. (California: SAGE Publications, Inc, 2011).
4. Ohmae, *The Borderless World*, Rev Ed.
5. Saskia J. Sassen, *Cities in a World Economy*, 4th ed. (California: SAGE Publications, Inc, 2011).
6. Charles P. Kindleberger, *The Formation of Financial Centers: A Study in Comparative Economic History (Princeton Studies in International Finance No. 36)*, 1st ed. (New Jersey: Princeton University Press, 1974); E.P. Davis, "International Financial Centres — An Industrial Analysis," Bank of England Discussion Paper, (September 1990); Richard Roberts, ed., *International Financial Centres* (Edward Elgar Pub, 1994); Youssef Cassis, *Capitals of Capital: The Rise and Fall of International Financial Centres 1780–2009* (Cambridge: Cambridge University Press, 2010); Sassen, *Cities in a World Economy*; J. J. Woo, *Business and Politics in Asia's Key Financial Centres — Hong Kong, Singapore and Shanghai*, 1st ed. (Singapore: Springer, 2016).
7. Sanchita Basu Das, *Road to Recovery: Singapore's Journey through the Global Crisis* (Singapore: Institute of Southeast Asian Studies, 2010).
8. Claire Cockerton, "Nurturing New FinTech Communities," in *The FinTech Book*, ed. Susanne Chishti and Janos Barberis (New York, N.Y.: John Wiley & Sons, Ltd,

2016), pp. 42–44, http://onlinelibrary.wiley.com/doi/10.1002/9781119218906.ch10/summary; J. J. Woo, *Singapore as an International Financial Centre: History, Politics and Policy* (London: Palgrave Macmillan, 2016).

9. Kam-Hon Lee and Ilan Vertinsky, "Strategic Adjustment of International Financial Centres (IFCs) in Small Economies: A Comparative Study of Hong Kong and Singapore," *Journal of Business Administration* 17, No. 1–2 (1988): 151–172; J. J. Woo, "Policy Relations and Policy Subsystems: Financial Policy in Hong Kong and Singapore," *International Journal of Public Administration* 38, No. 8 (2015): 553–561.
10. J. J. Woo, *Singapore as an International Financial Centre: History, Politics and Policy.*
11. Robert Geyer and Samir Rihani, *Complexity and Public Policy: A New Approach to 21st Century Politics, Policy And Society* (London; New York: Routledge, 2010); Peter Ho, "Governing for the Future: What Governments Can Do," RSIS Working Paper, 2012; Peter Ho, "Coping with Complexity," Insights & Publications (Singapore: McKinsey & Company, October 2012); David Colander and Roland Kupers, *Complexity and the Art of Public Policy: Solving Society's Problems from the Bottom Up* (Princeton, N.J.: Princeton University Press, 2014).
12. B. Guy Peters, "The Policy Capacity of Government," Research Paper (Canada: Canadian Centre for Management Development, 1996); Martin Painter and Jon Pierre, "Unpacking Policy Capacity: Issues and Themes," in *Challenges to State Policy Capacity: Global Trends and Comparative Perspectives*, ed. Martin Painter and Jon Pierre (Basingstoke: Palgrave Macmillan, 2005), pp. 1–18; Michael Howlett, "Policy Analytical Capacity and Evidence-Based Policy-Making: Lessons from Canada," *Canadian Public Administration* 52, No. 2 (2009): 153–175; Deborah Gleeson *et al.*, "Negotiating Tensions in Developing Organizational Policy Capacity: Comparative Lessons to Be Drawn," *Journal of Comparative Policy Analysis: Research and Practice* 13, No. 3 (June 1, 2011): 237–263; Louis W. Pauly and Bruce W. Jentleson, "Political Authority, Policy Capacity, and Twenty-First Century Governance," in *Political Authority and Policy Capacity in the Global System*, ed. Louis W. Pauly and Bruce W. Jentleson (New York, N.Y.: Routledge, 2014), pp. 3–15; B. Guy Peters, "Policy Capacity in Public Administration," *Policy and Society* 34, No. 3–4 (2015): 219–228, doi:10.1016/j.polsoc.2015.09.005; M. Howlett, "Policy Analytical Capacity: The Supply and Demand for Policy Analysis in Government," *Policy and Society* 34, No. 3–4 (2015): 173–182, doi:10.1016/j.polsoc.2015.09.002; Xun Wu, M. Ramesh, and Michael Howlett, "Blending Skill and Resources Across Multiple Levels of Activity: Competences, Capabilities and the Policy Capacities of Government," *Policy & Society* 34, No. 3–4 (2015): 165–171.
13. J. J. Woo *et al.*, "Dynamics of Global Financial Governance: Constraints, Opportunities, and Capacities in Asia," *Policy and Society*, Institutional and Policy Design for the Financial Sector, 35, No. 3 (September 2016): 269–282, doi:10.1016/j.polsoc.2016.10.002.

14. J. J. Woo, "Policy Relations and Policy Subsystems: Financial Policy in Hong Kong and Singapore"; J. J. Woo, M. Ramesh, and Michael Howlett, "Legitimation Capacity: System-Level Resources and Political Skills in Public Policy," *Policy & Society* 34, No. 3–4 (2015): 271–283.
15. Giliberto Capano and Jun Jie Woo, "Resilience and Robustness in Policy Design: A Critical Appraisal," *Policy Sciences*, January 5, 2017, pp. 1–28, doi:10.1007/s11077-016-9273-x.

Bibliography

Ames, Ben. "Post-Panamax Containerships Reach East Coast Ports — DC Velocity." *DC Velocity*, July 14, 2016. http://www.dcvelocity.com/articles/20160714-post-panamax-containerships-reach-east-coast-ports/.

ASEAN. "History." ASEAN Website. *ASEAN/ONE VISION ONE IDENTITY ONE COMMUNITY*, 2016. http://asean.org/asean/about-asean/history/.

Austin, Ian Patrick. *Goh Keng Swee and Southeast Asian Governance*. Singapore: Marshall Cavendish Academic, 2004.

Azhar, Saeed, and Marius Zaharia. "In Race to Be Asia's Fintech Hub, Singapore Leads Hong Kong." *Reuters*, July 3, 2016. http://www.reuters.com/article/us-singapore-fintech-idUSKCN0ZJ10P.

Baker, Andrew. "Restraining Regulatory Capture? Anglo-America, Crisis Politics and Trajectories of Change in Global Financial Governance." *International Affairs* 86, No. 3 (2010): 647–663.

Barinka, Alex. "IBM's Watson to Help Rich DBS Clients with 'Jeopardy' Smarts." *Bloomberg.com*, January 9, 2014. https://www.bloomberg.com/news/articles/2014-01-09/ibm-carves-out-1-billion-new-unit-for-jeopardy-champ-watson.

Beck, Thorsten, Ross Levine, and Norman Loayza. "Finance and the Sources of Growth." *Journal of Financial Economics* 58, No. 1–2 (2000): 261–300.

Beijing Review. "Shanghai FTZ: One Year On — Beijing Review." *Beijing Review*, 2016. http://www.bjreview.com.cn/Cover_Stories_Series_2014/shanghai_ftz_one_year_on.html.

Bó, Ernesto Dal. "Regulatory Capture: A Review." *Oxford Review of Economic Policy* 22, No. 2 (June 20, 2006): 203–225.

Brandes, Dennis, Cyrill Fischer, Michael Grampp, Michele Salvi, and Michael Walterman. "Deloitte Global Wealth Management Centre Ranking 2015." Zurich, Switzerland: Deloitte Consulting AG, 2015.

Brenner, Neil. "Globalisation as Reterritorialisation: The Re-Scaling of Urban Governance in the European Union." *Urban Studies* 36, No. 3 (March 1, 1999): 431–451. doi:10.1080/0042098993466.

Caballero-Anthony, Mely. "Understanding ASEAN's Centrality: Bases and Prospects in an Evolving Regional Architecture." *The Pacific Review* 27, No. 4 (August 8, 2014): 563–584. doi:10.1080/09512748.2014.924227.

Capano, Giliberto, and Jun Jie Woo. "Resilience and Robustness in Policy Design: A Critical Appraisal." *Policy Sciences*, January 5, 2017, pp. 1–28. doi:10.1007/s11077-016-9273-x.

Carney, Richard W. *Contested Capitalism: The Political Origins of Financial Institutions*. London: Routledge, 2010.

Carney, Richard W. "The Political Economy of Financial Systems." SSRN Scholarly Paper. Rochester, NY: Social Science Research Network, November 1, 2001. http://papers.ssrn.com/abstract=2165154.

Carroll, Toby, and Darryl S.L. Jarvis. "Introduction: Financialisation and Development in Asia under Late Capitalism." *Asian Studies Review* 38, No. 4 (October 2, 2014): 533–543.

Cassis, Youssef. *Capitals of Capital: The Rise and Fall of International Financial Centres 1780–2009*. Cambridge: Cambridge University Press, 2010.

Central Provident Fund Board. "CPFIS." *CPF Website*, September 7, 2016. https://www.cpf.gov.sg/members/bptopics/bp-topics/cpfis.

Cerny, Philip G. "The Dynamics of Financial Globalization: Technology, Market Structure, and Policy Response." *Policy Sciences* 27, No. 4 (1994): 319–342. doi:10.1007/BF01000063.

———. "The Political Economy of International Finance." In *Finance and World Politics: Markets, Regimes and States in the Post-Hegemonic Era*, edited by Philip G. Cerny, pp. 3–19. Aldershot: Edward Elgar Publishing Limited, 1993.

Chanjaroen, Chanyaporn, and Darren Boey. "Singapore Is Beating Hong Kong in Asia's Fintech Race." *Bloomberg*. December 7, 2016. https://www.bloomberg.com/news/articles/2016-12-07/with-fintech-rising-hong-kong-singapore-rivalry-gets-new-twist.

Channel NewsAsia. "Singapore E-Commerce Market to Exceed S$7b in 2025: Report." *Channel NewsAsia*, May 24, 2016. http://www.channelnewsasia.com/news/business/singapore-e-commerce/2811118.html.

———. "Singapore's General Insurance Industry Saw Premiums Rise to S$3.6b in 2015." *Channel NewsAsia*, March 17, 2016. http://www.channelnewsasia.com/news/business/singapore/singapore-s-general/2610590.html.

Chen, Sharon, and Chanyaporn Chanjaroen. "Singapore to Regulate Fintech Firms Only When They Pose Risk." *Bloomberg*, April 13, 2016. http://www.bloomberg.com/news/articles/2016-04-13/singapore-to-regulate-fintech-firms-only-when-they-pose-risks.

Chia, Der Jiun. "Objectives and Principles of Financial Supervision in Singapore." In *Regulation and the Limits of Competition*, pp. 44–58. Economics Symposium Series 1. Singapore: SNP International Publishing Pte. Ltd., 2007.

Citi. "Digital Disruption: How FinTech Is Forcing Banks to a Tipping Point." *Citi GPS: Global Perspectives & Solutions*. New York, N.Y.: Citigroup, March 2016.

Claessens, Stijn, and Laura Kodres. "The Regulatory Responses to the Global Financial Crisis: Some Uncomfortable Questions." *IMF Working Paper*. Washington, D.C.: International Monetary Fund, March 2014.

Claessens, Stijn, Mr M. Ayhan Kose, Mr Luc Laeven, and Fabian Valencia. *Financial Crises: Causes, Consequences, and Policy Responses*. International Monetary Fund, 2014.

Cockerton, Claire. "Nurturing New FinTech Communities." In *The FinTech Book*, edited by Susanne Chishti and Janos Barberis, pp. 42–44. New York, N.Y.: John Wiley & Sons, Ltd, 2016. http://onlinelibrary.wiley.com/doi/10.1002/9781119218906.ch10/summary.

Colander, David, and Roland Kupers. *Complexity and the Art of Public Policy: Solving Society's Problems from the Bottom Up*. Princeton, N.J.: Princeton University Press, 2014.

Committee on the Future of Economy Secretariat. "Committee On the Future Economy to Review Singapore's Economic Strategies and Position Us for The Future." Press Release. Singapore: Ministry of Finance, December 21, 2015. http://www.mof.gov.sg/news-reader/articleid/1565/parentId/59/year/2015?category=Press%20Releases.

Cunha, Derek Da. *Breakthrough: Roadmap for Singapore's Political Future*. Singapore: Straits Times Press Reference, 2012.

Cutler, A. Claire, Virginia Haufler, and Tony Porter. *Private Authority and International Affairs*. Albany: State University of New York Press, 1999.

Das, Sanchita Basu. *Road to Recovery: Singapore's Journey through the Global Crisis*. Singapore: Institute of Southeast Asian Studies, 2010.

Davis, E.P. "International Financial Centres — An Industrial Analysis." Bank of England Discussion Paper, September 1990.

Demirguc-Kunt, Asli, and Ross Levine. "Finance, Financial Sector Policies, And Long-Run Growth." *Research Working Papers* 1, No. 1 (2008): 1–82.

Department of Statistics Singapore. "Share of GDP by Industry," February 25, 2016. http://www.singstat.gov.sg/statistics/visualising-data/charts/share-of-gdp-by-industry.

Drezner, Daniel W. "Globalization and Policy Convergence." *International Studies Review* 3, No. 1 (January 1, 2001): 53–78.

Economic Development Board. "Facts and Rankings." *Singapore Economic Development Board — Investing Business in Singapore*, November 9, 2015. /content/edb/en/why-singapore/about-singapore/facts-and-rankings/rankings.html.

———. "Industries — Logistics and Supply Chain Management." *Singapore Economic Development Board — Investing Business in Singapore*, October 2, 2015. /content/edb/en/industries/industries/logistics-and-supply-chain-management.html.

Economic Review Committee. "Positioning Singapore as a Pre-Eminent Financial Centre in Asia." *Financial Services Working Group Report*. Singapore: Ministry of Trade and Industry, 2003.

Epstein, Gerald A. *Financialization and the World Economy*. Cheltenham, UK: Edward Elgar Publishing, 2005.

ETH. "KOF Index of Globalization 2016." KOF Index of Globalization. Zurich, Switzerland: ETH, 2016.

EY. "UK FinTech On the Cutting Edge an Evaluation of the International FinTech Sector." London, U.K.: EY, 2016.

Finextra. "ANZ and DBS Open New Labs to Coincide with Singapore Fintech Festival." *Finextra Research*, November 14, 2016. https://www.finextra.com/newsarticle/29756/anz-and-dbs-open-new-labs-to-coincide-with-singapore-fintech-festival.

Forrest, Ray, and Yosuke Hirayama. "The Financialisation of the Social Project: Embedded Liberalism, Neoliberalism and Home Ownership." *Urban Studies*, April 3, 2014. http://usj.sagepub.com/content/early/2014/04/02/0042098014528394.

Friedman, John. "The World City Hypothesis." In *The City: The City in Global Context*, edited by Michael Pacione, pp. 151–163. London: Routledge, 2002.

Friedman, Thomas L. *The World Is Flat: A Brief History of the Twenty-First Century*. 1st ed. New York: Farrar, Straus and Giroux, 2005.

Fukuyama, Francis. *State-Building: Governance and World Order in the 21st Century*. Ithaca, N.Y: Cornell University Press, 2004.

Gady, Franz-Stefan. "Singapore's Defense Budget Climbs 5.7 Percent." *The Diplomat*, March 19, 2015. http://thediplomat.com/2015/03/singapores-defense-budget-climbs-5-7-percent/.

Gehrig, Thomas. "Cities and the Geography of Financial Centers." In *Economies of Cities: Theoretical Perspectives*, edited by Jean-Marie Huriot and Jacques-Francois Thiesse, pp. 415–446. Cambridge: Cambridge University Press, 2000.

Geyer, Robert, and Samir Rihani. *Complexity and Public Policy: A New Approach to 21st Century Politics, Policy and Society*. London; New York: Routledge, 2010.

Gleeson, Deborah, David Legge, Deirdre O'Neill, and Monica Pfeffer. "Negotiating Tensions in Developing Organizational Policy Capacity: Comparative Lessons to Be Drawn." *Journal of Comparative Policy Analysis: Research and Practice* 13, No. 3 (June 1, 2011): 237–263.

Gnirck, Markus, and Gerben Visser. "Singapore, the FinTech Hub for Southeast Asia." In *The FinTech Book*, edited by Susanne Chishti and Janos Barberis, pp. 58–60. John Wiley & Sons, Ltd, 2016. http://onlinelibrary.wiley.com/doi/10.1002/9781119218906.ch16/summary.

Government of Singapore. "Mobile Penetration Rate." *Data.gov.sg*, December 14, 2016. https://data.gov.sg/dataset/mobile-penetration-rate.

———. "Number of Broadband Subscriptions by Type, Annual." *Data.gov.sg*, December 14, 2016. https://data.gov.sg/dataset/number-of-broadband-subscriptions-by-type-annual?resource_id=949a1766-8b8a-438f-8d61-c70173cb6c58.

Guo, Yvonne, and J. J. Woo. *Singapore and Switzerland: Secrets to Small State Success*. New Jersey: World Scientific Publishing Co., 2016.

Guo, Yvonne, and Jun Jie Woo. "Wealth Management for All Seasons." *The Straits Times*. December 3, 2013. http://www.academia.edu/6087604/Wealth_Management_for_All_Seasons.

Haggard, Stephen, and Chung H. Lee. "The Political Dimension of Finance in Economic Development." In *The Politics of Finance in Developing Countries*, edited by Stephen Haggard, Chung H. Lee, and Sylvia Maxfield, pp. 3–20. New York: Cornell University Press, 1993.

Haggard, Stephen, Chung H. Lee, and Sylvia Maxfield. *The Politics of Finance in Developing Countries*. Cornell University Press, 1993.

Hall, Peter Geoffrey. *The World Cities*. New York: McGraw-Hill, 1966.

Hall, Sarah. "Geographies of Money and Finance II: Financialization and Financial Subjects." *Progress in Human Geography* 36, No. 3 (2012): 403–411.

Hamilton-Hart, Natasha. *Asian States, Asian Bankers: Central Banking in Southeast Asia*. New York: Cornell University Press, 2002.

Haque, M. Shamsul. "Governance and Bureaucracy in Singapore: Contemporary Reforms and Implications." *International Political Science Review* 25, No. 2 (April 1, 2004): 227–240.

———. "Structures of New Public Management in Malaysia and Singapore: Alternative Views." *The Journal of Comparative Asian Development* 1, No. 1 (2002): 71–86.

Heng, Janice. "Fresh Graduates Banking on Finance Sector for Jobs." *The Straits Times*. July 8, 2013. http://www.straitstimes.com/singapore/fresh-graduates-banking-on-finance-sector-for-jobs.

Hinata-Yamaguchi, Ryo. "Singapore's Military Modernization." *The Diplomat*, April 27, 2012. http://thediplomat.com/2012/04/singapores-military-modernization/.

Ho, Peter. "Coping with Complexity." Insights & Publications. Singapore: McKinsey & Company, October 2012.

———. "Governing for the Future: What Governments Can Do." RSIS Working Paper, 2012.

Howlett, M. "Policy Analytical Capacity: The Supply and Demand for Policy Analysis in Government." *Policy and Society* 34, No. 3–4 (2015): 173–182. doi:10.1016/j.polsoc.2015.09.002.

Howlett, Michael. "Policy Analytical Capacity and Evidence-Based Policy-Making: Lessons from Canada." *Canadian Public Administration* 52, No. 2 (2009): 153–175.

Howlett, Michael, and Raul P. Lejano. "Tales From the Crypt The Rise and Fall (and Rebirth?) Of Policy Design." *Administration & Society* 45, No. 3 (April 1, 2013): 357–381.

Huff, W.G. "The Developmental State, Government, and Singapore's Economic Development since 1960." *World Development* 23, No. 8 (August 1995): 1421–1438.

IMD. "World Competitiveness Yearbook 2016." Lausanne: IMD, 2016.

Infocomm Development Authority of Singapore. "Singapore Lays Groundwork to Be World's First Smart Nation." News Release. Singapore: Infocomm Development Authority of Singapore, June 18, 2014. http://www.ida.gov.sg/blog/insg/featured/singapore-lays-groundwork-to-be-worlds-first-smart-nation/.

———. "Telecommunications." *Infocomm Development Authority of Singapore Website*, 2016. https://www.ida.gov.sg/Tech-Scene-News/Facts-and-Figures/Telecommunications.

International Enterprise Singapore. "Singapore FTAs — Trade from Singapore," 2016. http://www.iesingapore.gov.sg/Trade-From-Singapore/International-Agreements/free-trade-agreements/Singapore-FTA.

Investopedia. "Fintech." *Investopedia*, March 17, 2015. http://www.investopedia.com/terms/f/fintech.asp.

Jayaratne, Jith, and Philip E. Strahan. "The Finance-Growth Nexus: Evidence from Bank Branch Deregulation." *The Quarterly Journal of Economics* 111, No. 3 (August 1, 1996): 639–670.

Kear, Mark. "Governing Homo Subprimicus: Beyond Financial Citizenship, Exclusion, and Rights." *Antipode* 45, No. 4 (September 1, 2013): 926–946.

Kindleberger, Charles P. *The Formation of Financial Centers: A Study in Comparative Economic History (Princeton Studies in International Finance No. 36).* 1st ed. New Jersey: Princeton University Press, 1974.

King, Robert G., and Ross Levine. "Finance and Growth: Schumpeter Might Be Right." *The Quarterly Journal of Economics* 108, No. 3 (August 1, 1993): 717–737.

Koh, Jeremy. "New Asean Economic Community could give Singapore GDP a 9.5% boost by 2030: HSBC." *The Straits Times*. November 23, 2015. http://www.straitstimes.com/business/economy/new-asean-economic-community-could-give-singapore-gdp-a-95-boost-by-2030-hsbc.

Koh, Yong Guan. Interview, August 7, 2013.

Konstadakopulos, Dimitrios. *Learning for Innovation in the Global Knowledge Economy: A European and South-East Asian Perspective*. Bristol, U.K.: Intellect Books, 2004.

Kose, M. Ayhan, Eswar Prasad, Kenneth Rogoff, and Shang-Jin Wei. "Financial Globalization and Economic Policies." Discussion Paper Series. Bonn, Germany: Institute for the Study of Labor, February 2009.

Krippner, Greta R. "The Financialization of the American Economy." *Socio-Economic Review* 3, No. 2 (May 1, 2005): 173–208.

Laffont, Jean-Jacques, and Jean Tirole. "The Politics of Government Decision-Making: A Theory of Regulatory Capture." *The Quarterly Journal of Economics* 106, No. 4 (1991): 1089–1127. doi:10.2307/2937958.

Lai, Karen P Y. "Financial Advisors, Financial Ecologies and the Variegated Financialisation of Everyday Investors." *Transactions of the Institute of British Geographers* 41, No. 1 (January 1, 2016): 27–40. doi:10.1111/tran.12101.

———. "The Lehman Minibonds Crisis and Financialisation of Investor Subjects in Singapore." *Area* 45, No. 3 (September 1, 2013): 273–282. doi:10.1111/area.12040.

Lai, Karen P. Y., and Choon Hang Tan. "'Neighbours First, Bankers Second': Mobilising Financial Citizenship in Singapore." *Geoforum* 64 (August 2015): 65–77.

Lai, Karen P.Y. "Singapore's Economic Landscapes: Local Transformations and Global Networks." In *Changing Landscapes of Singapore: Old Tensions, New Discoveries*, edited by Elaine Lynn-Ee Ho, Yuan Woon Chih, and Kamalini Ramdas, pp. 196–217. Singapore: NUS Press, 2013.

Lee, Eliza W. Y., and M. Shamsul Haque. "The New Public Management Reform and Governance in Asian NICs: A Comparison of Hong Kong and Singapore." *Governance* 19, No. 4 (2006): 605–626.

Lee, Hsien Loong. "New Approach to Regulating and Developing Singapore's Financial Sector." Speech by DPM Lee Hsien Loong presented at the SESDAQ 10th Anniversary Dinner, Singapore, November 4, 1997.

———. "Smart Nation: Better Living, More Opportunities, Stronger Communities." presented at the Prime Minister Lee Hsien Loong's speech at Smart Nation launch, Singapore, November 24, 2014.

Lee, James. "Developmentalism, Social Welfare and State Capacity in East Asia: Integrating Housing and Social Security in Singapore." *Journal of Asian Public Policy* 2, No. 2 (2009): 157–170. doi:10.1080/17516230903027880.

Lee, Kam-Hon, and Ilan Vertinsky. "Strategic Adjustment of International Financial Centres (IFCs) in Small Economies: A Comparative Study of Hong Kong and Singapore." *Journal of Business Administration* 17, No. 1–2 (1988): 151 172.

Lee, Kuan Yew. *From Third World to First: The Singapore Story: 1965–2000*. Singapore: Times Editions, 2000.

Lee, Roger, and Ulrich Schmidt-Marwede. "Interurban Competition? Financial Centres and the Geography of Financial Production." *International Journal of Urban and Regional Research* 17, No. 4 (1993): 492–515.

Leifer, Michael. *Singapore's Foreign Policy: Coping with Vulnerability*. London: Routledge, 2000.

Levine, Michael E., and Jennifer L. Forrence. "Regulatory Capture, Public Interest, and the Public Agenda: Toward a Synthesis." *Journal of Law, Economics, & Organization* 6 (1990): 167–198.

Lim, Linda Y. C. "Fifty Years of Development in the Singapore Economy: An Introductory Review." *The Singapore Economic Review* 60, No. 3 (August 1, 2015): 1502002. doi:10.1142/S0217590815020026.

Low, Linda. "Globalisation and the Political Economy of Singapore's Policy on Foreign Talent and High Skills." *Journal of Education and Work* 15, No. 4 (December 1, 2002): 409–425. doi:10.1080/1363908022000023551.

———. *The Political Economy of a City-State: Government-Made Singapore*. Oxford: Oxford University Press, 2001.

———. *The Political Economy of a City-State Revised*. Singapore: Marshall Cavendish, 2006.

———. "The Singapore Developmental State in the New Economy and Polity." *The Pacific Review* 14, No. 3 (January 1, 2001): 411–441.

Mauzy, Diane K., and R. S. Milne. *Singapore Politics Under the People's Action Party*. 1 edition. London; New York: Routledge, 2002.

Menon, Ravi. "A Smart Financial Centre." Keynote Address presented at the Global Technology Law Conference 2015, Singapore, June 29, 2015. http://www.mas.gov.sg/news-and-publications/speeches-and-monetary-policy-statements/speeches/2015/a-smart-financial-centre.aspx.

———. Interview, September 26, 2013.

———. "Singapore's Financial Centre in the New Landscape." presented at the Investment Management Association of Singapore (IMAS) 14th Annual Conference, Singapore, March 13, 2013. http://www.mas.gov.sg/News-and-Publications/Monetary-Policy-Statements-and-Speeches/2013/Singapore-Financial-Centre-in-the-New-Landscape.aspx.

Meyer, John W. "Globalization Sources and Effects on National States and Societies." *International Sociology* 15, No. 2 (June 1, 2000): 233–248. doi:10.1177/02685809000 15002006.

Michailidou, Domna M. *The Inexorable Evolution of Financialisation: Financial Crises in Emerging Markets*. London: Palgrave Macmillan, 2016.

Ministry of Manpower. "Distribution of Employment by Industry." *Ministry of Manpower Singapore*, September 21, 2016. http://stats.mom.gov.sg/Pages/Employment-Distribution-and-Employment-Level-by-Industry.aspx.

———. "Summary Table: Employment." *Ministry of Manpower Singapore*, September 14, 2016. http://stats.mom.gov.sg/Pages/Employment-Summary-Table.aspx.

Ministry of Trade and Industry. "Do Free Trade Agreements Matter? Evaluating the Impact of FTAs on Singapore's Domestic Exports of Goods." Feature Article. Singapore: Ministry of Trade and Industry, 2011.

Monetary Authority of Singapore. "2000 Survey of the Singapore Asset Management Industry." Singapore: Monetary Authority of Singapore, 2000.

———. "2015 Singapore Asset Management Survey: Singapore — Global City, World of Opportunities." Singapore: Monetary Authority of Singapore, 2015.

———. "Financial Directory." *MASNET*, December 7, 2016. https://masnetsvc.mas.gov.sg/FID.html.

———. "Insurance Statistics 2015," November 26, 2016. http://www.mas.gov.sg/Statistics/Insurance-Statistics/Annual-Statistics/Insurance-Statistics-2015.aspx.

———. "MAS Establishes FinTech Innovation Lab." Press Release. Singapore: Monetary Authority of Singapore, August 24, 2016. http://www.mas.gov.sg/News-and-Publications/Media-Releases/2016/MAS-establishes-FinTech-Innovation-Lab.aspx.

———. "MAS FinTech Regulatory Sandbox." *MAS Website*, November 26, 2016. http://www.mas.gov.sg/Singapore-Financial-Centre/Smart-Financial-Centre/FinTech-Regulatory-Sandbox.aspx.

———. "MAS Sets up New FinTech and Innovation Group." *MAS Website*, November 26, 2016. http://www.mas.gov.sg/news-and-publications/media-releases/2015/mas-sets-up-new-fintech-and-innovation-group.aspx.

Montes, Manuel F. "Tokyo, Hong Kong and Singapore as Competing Financial Centres." *Journal of Asian Business* 18, No. 1 (1999): 153–168.

Mulcahy, Niamh. "Entrepreneurial Subjectivity and the Political Economy of Daily Life in the Time of Finance." *European Journal of Social Theory*, June 21, 2016, 1368431016655074. doi:10.1177/1368431016655074.

National Library Board Singapore. "Establishment of the Economic Review Committee — Singapore History." *History SG*, 2016. http://eresources.nlb.gov.sg/history/events/459b32e3-35c3-4112-9042-94aaa9c13057.

Oatley, Thomas, W. Kindred Winecoff, Andrew Pennock, and Sarah Bauerle Danzman. "The Political Economy of Global Finance: A Network Model." *Perspectives on Politics* 11, No. 1 (2013): 133–153.

Ohmae, Kenichi. *The Borderless World, Rev Ed: Power and Strategy in the Interlinked Economy*. Revised ed. New York: HarperBusiness, 1999.

Olds, Kris, and Henry Yeung. "Pathways to Global City Formation: A View from the Developmental City-State of Singapore." *Review of International Political Economy* 11, No. 3 (June 1, 2004): 489–521. doi:10.1080/0969229042000252873.

O'Rourke, Kevin H., and Jeffrey G. Williamson. "When Did Globalisation Begin?" *European Review of Economic History* 6, No. 1 (April 1, 2002): 23–50. doi:10.1017/S1361491602000023.

Painter, Martin, and Jon Pierre. "Unpacking Policy Capacity: Issues and Themes." In *Challenges to State Policy Capacity: Global Trends and Comparative Perspectives*, edited by Martin Painter and Jon Pierre, pp. 1–18. Basingstoke: Palgrave Macmillan, 2005.

Palmioli, Giovanni, and Adam Heal. "Structural Economic Reform in China: The Role of the Shanghai Free Trade Zone." Trade Insights. Washington, D.C: UNESCAP, November 2014.

Pauly, Louis W., and Bruce W. Jentleson. "Political Authority, Policy Capacity, and Twenty-First Century Governance." In *Political Authority and Policy Capacity in the Global System*, edited by Louis W. Pauly and Bruce W. Jentleson, pp. 3–15. New York, N.Y.: Routledge, 2014.

Pereira, Alexius. "Singapore's Regionalization Strategy." *Journal of the Asia Pacific Economy* 10, No. 3 (January 1, 2005): 380–396. doi:10.1080/13547860500163480.

Perry, Martin. *Singapore: A Developmental City State*. Chichester: Wiley, 1997.

Peters, B. Guy. "Policy Capacity in Public Administration." *Policy and Society* 34, No. 3–4 (2015): 219–228. doi:10.1016/j.polsoc.2015.09.005.

———. "The Policy Capacity of Government." Research Paper. Canada: Canadian Centre for Management Development, 1996.

Prasad, Eswar, Kenneth Rogoff, Shang-Jin Wei, and M. Ayhan Kose. "Effects of Financial Globalization on Developing Countries: Some Empirical Evidence." Washington, D.C.: International Monetary Fund, March 17, 2003.

Putzel, James. "Globalization, Liberalization, and Prospects for the State." *International Political Science Review* 26, No. 1 (January 1, 2005): 5–16. doi:10.1177/0192512105047893.

Quah, Jon S. T. *Public Administration Singapore-Style*. Singapore: Emerald Group Publishing, 2010.

Rajaratnam, S. "Global City' Success for Spore: Raja." *The Straits Times*. February 7, 1972.

Ramesh, M. "Economic Globalization and Policy Choices." *Governance: An International Journal of Policy and Administration* 8, No. 2 (1995): 243–260.

Ranasinghe, Dhara. "Singapore, the Tiny State with Military Clout." *CNBC*, February 9, 2014. http://www.cnbc.com/2014/02/07/singapore-the-tiny-state-with-military-clout.html.

Reed, Howard Curtis. *The Preeminence of International Financial Centers*. New York: Praeger, 1981.

Roberts, Richard, ed. *International Financial Centres*. Edward Elgar Pub, 1994.

Rodrik, Dani. *The Globalization Paradox: Democracy and the Future of the World Economy*. Reprint edition. New York; London: W. W. Norton & Company, 2012.

Rolls, Mark. "Centrality and Continuity: ASEAN and Regional Security since 1967." *East Asia* 29, No. 2 (June 1, 2012): 127–139. doi:10.1007/s12140-011-9160-1.

Sassen, Saskia. "Global Financial Centers." *Foreign Affairs* 78 (1999): 75–87.

———. *Global Networks, Linked Cities*. New York, NY, 10001: Routledge, 2001.

———. *Territory, Authority, Rights: From Medieval to Global Assemblages*. Updated ed. edition. Princeton, N.J.: Princeton University Press, 2008.

———. *The Global City: New York, London, Tokyo*. 2nd ed. Princeton, N.J: Princeton University Press, 2001.

———. "Whose City Is It? Globalization and the Formation of New Claims." *Public Culture* 8, No. 2 (1996): 205–223.

Sassen, Saskia J. *Cities in a World Economy*. Fourth Edition edition. California: SAGE Publications, Inc., 2011.

———. *De-Nationalization*. Princeton, N.J.: Princeton University Press, 2003.

Schmukler, Sergio L. "Benefits and Risks of Financial Globalization: Challenges for Developing Countries." Washington, D.C.: World Bank, June 2004.

Schwab, Klaus. "The Global Competitiveness Report 2015–2016." Geneva: World Economic Forum, 2016.

Shanmugaratnam, Tharman. "Speech at the Launch of the Singapore FinTech Festival." Speech presented at the Launch of the Singapore FinTech Festival at the Asia Society, New York, N.Y., April 12, 2016. http://www.mas.gov.sg/News-and-Publications/Speeches-and-Monetary-Policy-Statements/Speeches/2016/Speech-at-the-Launch-of-the-Singapore-FinTech-Festival.aspx.

Shen, Simon. "Why Singapore Plays a Pivotal Role in ASEAN." *EJ Insight*, April 20, 2015. http://www.ejinsight.com/20150420-singapore-pivotal-role-asean/.

Singh, Bilveer. *Politics and Governance in Singapore: An Introduction*. 2nd ed. Singapore: McGraw-Hill Education (Asia), 2012.

Smart Nation Programme Office. "About Smart Nation," 2016. http://www.smartnation.sg/about-smart-nation.

Stiglitz, Joseph E. *Globalization and Its Discontents*. New York: W.W. Norton, 2003.

Stiglitz, Joseph E. *Making Globalization Work*. Reprint edition. New York: W. W. Norton & Company, 2007.

Strange, Susan. *The Retreat of the State: The Diffusion of Power in the World Economy*. Cambridge: Cambridge University Press, 1996.

Tan, Kenneth Paul. "Singapore in 2011: A 'New Normal' in Politics?" *Asian Survey* 52, No. 1 (February 2012): 220–226.

———. "The Singapore Parliament: Representation, Effectiveness, and Control." In *Parliaments in Asia: Institutional Building and Political Development*, edited by Yongnian Zheng, Liang Fook Lye, and Wilheim Hofmeister, pp. 27–46. Oxford, U.K.: Routledge, 2013. https://www.academia.edu/5057723/Tan_Kenneth_Paul_The_Singapore_parliament_representation_effectiveness_and_control_._In_Parliaments_in_Asia_Institutional_Building_and_Political_Development_ed._Zheng_Yongnian_Lye_Liang_Fook_and_Wilhelm_Hofmeister._Oxford_Routledge_2013.

Tan, Nicole. "Singapore Economy Grew 2.1% in 2015, Beating Expectations." *Channel NewsAsia*. January 4, 2016, sec. Business. http://www.channelnewsasia.com/news/business/singapore-economy-grew-2/2396126.html.

Tang, See Kit. "Singapore's Manufacturing Output Falls 3.6% in July, First Contraction in 5 Months." *Channel NewsAsia*, August 26, 2016. http://www.channelnewsasia.com/news/business/singapore/singapore-s-manufacturing/3075904.html.

The Economist. "Singapore Tries to Become a Fintech Hub." *The Economist*, January 14, 2017. http://www.economist.com/news/finance-and-economics/21714384-city-state-wants-fintech-bolsters-not-disrupts-mainstream.

The Straits Times. "Singapore's Financial Services Sector Resilient amid New Challenges." *The Straits Times*. March 16, 2016.

Verhetsel, Ann, and Steve Sel. "World Maritime Cities: From Which Cities Do Container Shipping Companies Make Decisions?" *Transport Policy*, SI: TBGS The International Forum on Shipping, Ports and Airports (IFSPA) 2008, 16, No. 5 (September 2009): 240–250. doi:10.1016/j.tranpol.2009.08.002.

Wan, Zheng, Yang Zhang, Xuefeng Wang, and Jihong Chen. "Policy and Politics behind Shanghai's Free Trade Zone Program." *Journal of Transport Geography* 34 (January 2014): 1–6. doi:10.1016/j.jtrangeo.2013.10.015.

Wang, Jiangyu. "The Rise of Singapore as International Financial Centre: Political Will, Industrial Policy, and Rule of Law." In *Finance, Rule of Law and Development in Asia*, edited by Jiaxin Hu, Matthias Vanhullebusch, and Andrew Harding, pp. 1–17. Leiden: Brill Nijhoff, 2016. http://booksandjournals.brillonline.com/content/books/b9789004315815_002.

Warren, Neil. "Internet and Globalisation." In *Economics of Globalisation*, edited by Partha Gangopadhyay and Manas Chatterji, pp. 191–202. Aldershot: Ashgate Publishing, Ltd., 2005.

Wolf, Martin. *Why Globalization Works*. 2nd ed. New Haven: Yale University Press, 2005.

Wong, Kelvin. "Differentiate Your Business Through Supply Chain Optimisation." *Singapore Economic Development Board*, June 5, 2015. /content/edb/en/resources/downloads/articles/supply-chain-optimisation.html.

Wong, Wei Han. "Singapore's asset management industry grew strongly in 2014: MAS." *The Straits Times*, July 21, 2015. http://www.straitstimes.com/business/economy/singapores-asset-management-industry-grew-strongly-in-2014-mas.

Woo, J. J., M. Ramesh, Michael Howlett, and Mehmet Kerem Coban. "Dynamics of Global Financial Governance: Constraints, Opportunities, and Capacities in Asia." *Policy and Society*, Institutional and Policy Design for the Financial Sector, 35, No. 3 (September 2016): 269–282. doi:10.1016/j.polsoc.2016.10.002.

Woo, J. J. "Beyond the Neoliberal Orthodoxy: Alternative Financial Policy Regimes in Asia's Financial Centres." *Critical Policy Studies* 9, No. 3 (2015): 297–316.

———. *Business and Politics in Asia's Key Financial Centres — Hong Kong, Singapore and Shanghai*. 1st ed. Singapore: Springer, 2016.

———. "Policy Relations and Policy Subsystems: Financial Policy in Hong Kong and Singapore." *International Journal of Public Administration* 38, No. 8 (2015): 553–561.

———. *Singapore as an International Financial Centre: History, Politics and Policy*. London: Palgrave Macmillan, 2016.

———. "Singapore's Policy Style: Statutory Boards as Policymaking Units." *Journal of Asian Public Policy* 8, No. 2 (2014): 120–133.

Woo, J. J., M. Ramesh, and Michael Howlett. "Legitimation Capacity: System-Level Resources and Political Skills in Public Policy." *Policy & Society* 34, No. 3–4 (2015): 271–283.

Woo, Jun Jie. "Free Trade Zone Fits into Shanghai's Financial Ambition." *South China Morning Post*. July 20, 2013.

———. "Three Ts behind Singapore's Future as a Leading Financial Centre." *TODAY*. June 26, 2014. http://www.todayonline.com/business/three-ts-behind-singapores-future-leading-financial-centre.

Woo, Jun Jie, and Debbie Loo. "Sharing Solutions City-to-City." *TODAY*. May 29, 2014. http://www.todayonline.com/singapore/sharing-solutions-city-city.

World Bank. "Exports of Goods and Services (% of GDP)." Washington, D.C.: World Bank, 2016.

———. "Foreign Direct Investment, Net Inflows (% of GDP) | Data." *World Bank Database*, 2016. http://data.worldbank.org/indicator/BX.KLT.DINV.WD.GD.ZS?locations=SG&view=chart.

———. "GDP (Current US$) | Data." *World Bank Database*. Accessed September 23, 2016. http://data.worldbank.org/indicator/NY.GDP.MKTP.CD?locations=SG&view=chart.

———. "GDP per Capita (Current USS)." *World Bank Database*, 2016. http://data.worldbank.org/indicator/NY.GDP.PCAP.CD?locations=SG&view=chart.

———. "Service Exports." *World Bank Database*, 2016. http://data.worldbank.org/indicator/BX.GSR.NFSV.CD?locations=SG.

———. "Trade," 2016. http://data.worldbank.org/topic/trade?locations=SG.

Worsham, Jeff. *Other People's Money: Policy Change, Congress, And Bank Regulation*. Boulder, C.O.: Westview Press, 1997.

Wu, Xun, M. Ramesh, and Michael Howlett. "Blending Skill and Resources Across Multiple Levels of Activity: Competences, Capabilities and the Policy Capacities of Government." *Policy & Society* 34, No. 3–4 (2015): 165–171.

Yahya, Yasmine. "Singapore's push to be fintech hub." *The Straits Times*. November 22, 2016. http://www.straitstimes.com/business/companies-markets/singapores-push-to-be-fintech-hub.

Ye, Jing. "Decentralized Authorities and Transnational Policy Diffusion: The Case of Free Trade Zone in China." *World Economics and Policy*, No. 7 (2014). http://en.cnki.com.cn/Article_en/CJFDTotal-SJJZ201407009.htm.

Yeandle, Mark. "Global Financial Centre Index 19." London, U.K.: Z/Yen Group and Qatar Financial Centre Authority, March 2016.

———. "Global Financial Centres Index 17." London, U.K.: Z/Yen Group and Qatar Financial Centre Authority, March 2015.

———. "Global Financial Centres Index 18." London, U.K.: Z/Yen Group and Qatar Financial Centre Authority, September 2015.

Yeoh, Brenda, and Katie Willis. "The Global–Local Nexus: Singapore's Regionalisation Drive." *Geography* 82, No. 2 (1997): 183–186.

Yester, Katherine. "Measuring Globalization." *Foreign Policy*, November 20, 2009. https://foreignpolicy.com/2009/11/20/measuring-globalization/.

Yeung, Henry Wai-Chung. "State Intervention and Neoliberalism in the Globalizing World Economy: Lessons from Singapore's Regionalization Programme." *The Pacific Review* 13, No. 1 (January 1, 2000): 133–162. doi:10.1080/095127400363677.

Yeyati, Eduardo Levy, and Tomas Williams. *Financial Globalization in Emerging Economies: Much Ado about Nothing?* Policy Research Working Papers. Washington, D.C.: The World Bank, 2011. http://elibrary.worldbank.org/doi/abs/10.1596/1813-9450-5624.

Zhang, Xiaoyan, and Dafei Chen. "The Influence of Financial Industry Cluster on Economic Growth: Three Economic Zones in China." *Accounting and Finance Research* 2, No. 4 (October 13, 2013). doi:10.5430/afr.v2n4p69.

About the Author

J. J. Woo is an Assistant Professor in the Public Policy and Global Affairs Programme of the School of Social Sciences, Nanyang Technological University, Singapore. He is also Rajawali Fellow (2016–2017) at the John F. Kennedy School of Government, Harvard University. His current research focuses on the politics of development, global city formation, and urban policy.

Dr. Woo received his Ph.D. from the Lee Kuan Yew School of Public Policy, National University of Singapore, where he wrote a thesis on the policy mechanisms underlying the success of Asian financial centres such as Hong Kong, Singapore, and Shanghai. He holds a Master of Science in International Political Economy from the S. Rajaratnam School of International Studies, Nanyang Technological University, and First Class Honours in Economics and Business Management from the University of London.

An avid scholar of the global financial centre, Dr. Woo's other books on the subject include *Business and Politics in Asia's Key Financial Centres: Hong Kong, Singapore and Shanghai*

(Springer, 2015) and *Singapore as an International Financial Centre: History, Policy and Politics* (Palgrave Macmillan, 2016). He has also co-authored a book on comparative public policy, entitled *Singapore and Switzerland: Secrets to Small State Success*, published by World Scientific in 2016.

Aside from books, Dr. Woo has also published extensively in leading international peer-reviewed journals, such as *Policy Sciences*, *Policy and Politics*, *Critical Policy Studies*, and *Policy and Society*, among others. He recently presented a co-authored paper on cultural policy in the global city at the Ninth Architecture, Culture, and Society Forum (ACSF). His commentary pieces have appeared in leading national newspapers such as the *Straits Times*, *Business Times*, and *Today*.

In his free time, J. J. is an avid runner and dabbles in the philosophy of Ludwig Wittgenstein.